COPYRIGHT

BILLS OF LADING IN SHIPPING LAW
An Australian Perspective

Published by John Gates Books
International Trade and Transport Law Library – Book 2

The information in this book is provided for educational and informational purposes. While every effort has been made to ensure accuracy, the author and publisher make no representations or warranties regarding the completeness or accuracy of the contents. This book does not constitute legal advice. Readers should consult qualified legal professionals for specific legal matters.

National Library of Australia Cataloguing-in-Publication entry:
Gates, John
Bills of Lading in Shipping Law: An Australian Perspective / John Gates
1st ed.
ISBN: 978-1-7646-123-4-0 (hardcover)
ISBN: 978-1-7646-123-5-7 (paperback)

Subjects: Maritime law--Australia. Bills of lading. International trade--Law and legislation.
Shipping--Law and legislation. Carriage of goods by sea--Australia.

Cover design: Author
Printed in Australia

John Gates Books
johngates@outlook.com.au

First Edition, 2026

BILLS OF LADING IN SHIPPING LAW

An Australian Perspective

To the maritime professionals who keep global commerce moving.

ABOUT THE AUTHOR

John Gates has been an International Trade and Transport Lawyer, writer, blogger, and former Naval Officer with extensive experience across maritime operations and commercial law.

He currently consults to commercial organisations.

Before entering legal practice, he served as a Naval Officer, gaining firsthand experience in maritime operations, navigation, and vessel management. This operational background provides him with practical insights that inform his legal analysis and distinguishes his approach to shipping law.

Coming back to this field of endeavour, his first love, Gates intends to contribute more to maritime publications and maintain an authoritative presence in international trade law discourse.

His writing bridges the gap between academic rigor and practical application, making complex legal principles accessible to shipping professionals, lawyers, and students alike.

Gates is the creator and editor of the International Trade and Transport Law Library, a comprehensive series dedicated to examining critical aspects of maritime commerce, shipping documentation, and international trade regulation.

This is the second book in the International Trade Series, the first published in 2014, was "International Trade, the Ins and Outs of Import and Export".

Contents

TABLE OF AUTHORITIES

Cases, legislation, and other authorities are cited throughout the text following the Australian Guide to Legal Citation (4th ed). Full citations are provided where authorities are first referenced in each chapter.

CASES

Australian Cases

1. Ace Imports Pty Ltd v Lloyd Brasileiro (1987) 10 NSWLR 32
2. Akai Pty Ltd v People's Insurance Co Ltd (1996) 188 CLR 418
3. Carrington Slipways Pty Ltd v Patrick Operations Pty Ltd (1991) 24 NSWLR 745
4. El Greco (Australia) Pty Ltd v Mediterranean Shipping Co SA [2004] FCA 202
5. Hi-Fert Pty Ltd v Kiukiang Maritime Carriers Inc (No 5) (1998) 90 FCR 1
6. Kupang Setia Sdn Bhd v Bali Shipping Pte Ltd (2001) NSWSC (unreported)
7. Lakeport Navigation Co Panama SA v Waipawa Shipping Ltd (1992) 27 NSWLR 56
8. Mauritius Oil Refineries Ltd v Stolt-Nielsen Nederland BV (2004) 140 FCR 518
9. Port Jackson Stevedoring Pty Ltd v Salmond & Spraggon (Australia) Pty Ltd (The New York Star) (1978) 139 CLR 231
10. Shipping Corporation of India Ltd v Gamlen Chemical Co (A/Asia) Pty Ltd (1980) 147 CLR 142

English and Privy Council Cases

1. Albacora SRL v Westcott & Laurance Line Ltd [1966] 2 Lloyd's Rep 53
2. Brown Jenkinson & Co Ltd v Percy Dalton (London) Ltd [1957] 2 QB 621
3. Canada Rice Mills Ltd v Union Marine & General Insurance Co Ltd [1941] AC 55
4. Castellain v Preston (1883) 11 QBD 380
5. Elder, Dempster & Co v Paterson, Zochonis & Co [1924] AC 522
6. Freeman & Lockyer v Buckhurst Park Properties (Mangal) Ltd [1964] 2 QB 480
7. Gosse Millerd Ltd v Canadian Government Merchant Marine Ltd [1929] AC 223
8. Grant v Norway (1851) 10 CB 665
9. Interfoto Picture Library Ltd v Stiletto Visual Programmes Ltd [1989] QB 433
10. Leduc v Ward (1888) 20 QBD 475
11. Lennard's Carrying Co Ltd v Asiatic Petroleum Co Ltd [1915] AC 705

12. Lickbarrow v Mason (1787) 2 TR 63
13. Maxine Footwear Co Ltd v Canadian Government Merchant Marine Ltd [1959] AC 589
14. Motis Exports Ltd v Dampskibsselskabet AF 1912 [2000] 1 Lloyd's Rep 211
15. New Zealand Shipping Co Ltd v A.M. Satterthwaite & Co Ltd (The Eurymedon) [1975] AC 154
16. Scruttons Ltd v Midland Silicones Ltd [1962] AC 446
17. SS Ardennes (Cargo Owners) v SS Ardennes (Owners) [1951] 1 KB 55
18. Standard Chartered Bank v Pakistan National Shipping Corp [2002] UKHL 43
19. Sze Hai Tong Bank Ltd v Rambler Cycle Co Ltd [1959] AC 576
20. T.W. Thomas & Co Ltd v Portsea Steamship Co Ltd [1912] AC 1
21. The David Agmashenebeli [2003] 1 Lloyd's Rep 92
22. The Fal Estuary [1990] 2 Lloyd's Rep 191
23. The Hollandia [1983] 1 AC 565
24. The Varenna [1984] QB 599
25. V/O Rasnoimport v Guthrie & Co Ltd [1966] 1 Lloyd's Rep 1

LEGISLATION

Commonwealth Legislation

- Autonomous Sanctions Act 2011 (Cth)
- Carriage of Goods by Sea Act 1991 (Cth)
- Charter of the United Nations Act 1945 (Cth)
- Civil Liability (Third Party Claims Against Insurers) Act 2017 (Cth)
- Competition and Consumer Act 2010 (Cth)
- Corporations Act 2001 (Cth) • Criminal Code Act 1995 (Cth)
- Electronic Transactions Act 1999 (Cth)
- Hazardous Waste (Regulation of Exports and Imports) Act 1989 (Cth)
- Marine Insurance Act 1909 (Cth)
- Marine Safety (Domestic Commercial Vessel) National Law •
- Navigation Act 2012 (Cth)
- Personal Property Securities Act 2009 (Cth)
- Privacy Act 1988 (Cth)
- Sea-Carriage of Goods Act 1924 (Cth) [repealed]
- Security of Critical Infrastructure Act 2018 (Cth)

State Legislation

- Mercantile Law Act 1936 (SA)
- Sale of Goods Act 1923 (NSW)

- Sale of Goods Acts of Victoria, Queensland, Western Australia, Tasmania, Australian Capital Territory, and Northern Territory (equivalent provisions)

Imperial Legislation (Historical)

- Bills of Lading Act 1855 (Imp) (18 & 19 Vict c 111)

INTERNATIONAL CONVENTIONS AND INSTRUMENTS

Maritime Conventions

- Convention on the Contract for the International Carriage of Goods by Road (CMR), Geneva, 19 May 1956
- International Convention for the Safety of Life at Sea (SOLAS), 1 November 1974, as amended
- International Convention for the Unification of Certain Rules of Law relating to Bills of Lading (Hague Rules), Brussels, 25 August 1924
- International Convention on the Limitation of Liability for Maritime Claims, London, 19 November 1976
- Protocol Amending the International Convention (Hague-Visby Rules), Brussels, 23 February 1968
- Protocol Amending (SDR Protocol), Brussels, 21 December 1979
- United Nations Convention on Contracts for the International Carriage of Goods Wholly or Partly by Sea (Rotterdam Rules), Rotterdam, 23 September 2009
- United Nations Convention on the Carriage of Goods by Sea (Hamburg Rules), Hamburg, 31 March 1978
- Commercial Rules and Model Laws Incoterms 2020, ICC Publication No. 723
- International Maritime Dangerous Goods Code (IMDG Code), IMO
- UNCITRAL Model Law on Electronic Commerce (1996)
- UNCITRAL Model Law on Electronic Transferable Records (2017)
- Uniform Customs and Practice for Documentary Credits (UCP 600),
- ICC Publication No. 600
- York-Antwerp Rules 2016, CMI Standard Forms CONLINEBILL 2000 (BIMCO)
- CONGENBILL (BIMCO)
- Institute Cargo Clauses (A, B, C), IUA London

MULTIDOC 95 (BIMCO) BOOKS AND TREATISES

- Berlingieri, Francesco, International Maritime Conventions (Informa Law, 2014)
- Cooke, Julian et al, Voyage Charters (4th ed, Informa Law, 2014)

- Davies, Martin and Dickey, Anthony, Shipping Law (4th ed, Thomson Reuters, 2016)
- Gaskell, Nicholas et al, Bills of Lading: Law and Contracts (LLP, 2000)
- Scrutton, Thomas Edward, Scrutton on Charterparties and Bills of Lading (24th ed, Sweet & Maxwell, 2021)
- Tetley, William, Marine Cargo Claims (4th ed, Thomson Carswell, 2008)
- Treitel, G.H. and Reynolds, F.M.B., Carver on Bills of Lading (4th ed, Sweet & Maxwell, 2017)
- Wilson, John, Carriage of Goods by Sea (8th ed, Pearson, 2020)

OTHER AUTHORITIES

- Australian Guide to Legal Citation (4th ed, MULRA, 2018)
- Australian Business Law Review
- Australian Maritime Safety Authority Guidelines
- Digital Container Shipping Association Standards
- Federal Law Review
- International Maritime Organization Publications
- Journal of International Maritime Law
- Lloyd's Maritime and Commercial Law Quarterly
- Melbourne University Law Review
- Shipping and Trade Law
- Sydney Law Review
- United Nations Commission on International Trade Law Working Papers

PREFACE

Bills of lading are extraordinary documents. For centuries, they have enabled international trade by performing three functions simultaneously: they serve as receipts for goods shipped, evidence of contracts of carriage, and documents of title that allow goods to be bought, sold, and financed while crossing oceans. This unique character makes bills of lading indispensable to global commerce, yet their complexity often proves daunting even to experienced practitioners.

This book grew from a simple observation: while Australian shipping law is well-developed and sophisticated, no comprehensive treatise exists that examines bills of lading solely from an Australian legal perspective. Practitioners must consult UK texts, adapt international commentary, or piece together understanding from scattered case law and statute. This gap seemed increasingly problematic as shipping practice evolves, electronic documentation emerges, and new technologies reshape maritime commerce.

My approach to this subject has been shaped by dual perspectives. Before entering legal practice, I served as a Naval Officer, experiencing firsthand the operational realities of maritime transport—the challenge of loading cargo in difficult conditions, the anxiety of navigating heavy weather with valuable goods on board, the complexity of port operations under commercial pressure. These experiences informed my understanding that shipping law must serve practical needs while maintaining principled foundations.

Transitioning to legal practice deepened my appreciation for the sophisticated legal frameworks governing bills of lading. The Hague-Visby Rules, as implemented through the Carriage of Goods by Sea Act 1991 (Cth), represent a carefully balanced compromise between carrier and cargo interests. Australian case law has developed nuanced approaches to difficult questions about incorporation of charterparty terms, the evidential effect of receipt statements, and the scope of carrier exceptions. This body of law deserves comprehensive examination in an Australian context.

STRUCTURE AND APPROACH

This book progresses logically through ten chapters, each building on previous material. Chapter 1 introduces bills of lading and traces their historical development through various international conventions. Chapter 2 examines the three functions in detail, exploring how they interrelate and sometimes conflict. Chapters 3 and 4 address the practical aspects of types, forms, issue, and transfer.

Chapters 5, 6, and 7 provide in-depth analysis of each function: the receipt function (examining Article III rule 3 requirements and evidential effects), the contract evidence function (including the complex area of charterparty incorporation), and the document of title function (exploring its operation in sales, finance, and insurance). Chapter 8 addresses delivery obligations and the serious consequences of misdelivery. Chapter 9 examines carrier exceptions and limitations under the Hague-Visby Rules. Chapter 10 looks forward, addressing electronic bills, blockchain, autonomous vessels, and other contemporary developments.

Throughout, I have sought to integrate Australian statutory provisions, case law, and practical considerations. Every chapter references the Carriage of Goods by Sea Act 1991 (Cth) and related Commonwealth and State legislation. High Court, Federal Court, and State Supreme Court decisions are examined alongside influential English and Privy Council authorities. Where international conventions or foreign cases are discussed, their relevance to Australian practice is always explained.

AUDIENCE

This book serves multiple audiences. Legal practitioners handling maritime disputes or advising on international trade will find useful analysis of the legal principles governing bills of lading, supported by extensive case citations and statutory references. Shipping professionals—carriers, freight forwarders, ship managers, port operators—will find practical guidance on documentation requirements, liability issues, and risk management.

Trade finance bankers and documentary credit specialists will benefit from detailed examination of how bills function in letters of credit, the strict compliance doctrine, and the interplay between banking practice and shipping law. Marine insurance underwriters and claims handlers will find analysis of how bills create insurable interests, how insurance rights are assigned, and how carrier liability intersects with insurance coverage.

Law students studying maritime law, international trade law, or commercial law will find a comprehensive treatment suitable for coursework and examination preparation. The book assumes basic legal knowledge but explains specialised maritime concepts, making it accessible to those new to shipping law while providing depth for advanced study.

WHAT THIS BOOK IS NOT

This is not a practitioners' manual with precedent forms and step-by-step procedures, though practical guidance is provided throughout. It is not an international comparative study, though international developments are examined where relevant to Australian law. It is not a historical treatise, though historical context illuminates current law. Rather, this is a succinct legal analysis of bills of lading in Australian shipping law, combining doctrinal examination with practical application.

ACKNOWLEDGMENTS

This book would not exist without the foundation provided by scholars and practitioners who have developed shipping law over centuries. While I cannot acknowledge everyone who influenced my thinking, certain works deserve special mention. Martin Davies and Anthony Dickey's *Maritime Law in Australia* provided the model for rigorous Australian legal scholarship in this field. English authorities, particularly

Scrutton on Charterparties and Bills of Lading, Carver on Bills of Lading, and Gaskell on Bills of Lading, remain essential references that informed my analysis while I sought to provide distinctly Australian perspectives. I had the pleasure of meeting with Nick Gaskell at a summer school at the Institute of Maritime Law over 30 years ago.

My naval experience taught me the practical realities of shipping that no textbook can fully convey. My legal colleagues in my former maritime practice have sharpened my understanding through challenging cases and thoughtful discussions. Shipping clients who faced real problems required practical solutions that reconciled legal principle with commercial reality.

In recent times, I have taken on a logistics role in one of the companies that I consult to, which will involve International liner and breakbulk shipping, so I decided to re-educate myself and what better way than to pull out my notes and other data saved over the years, always intending to write, but never quite getting around to it. Thanks to some assistance from AI, I have now been able to organise myself to get the structure right and finish what I meant to start years ago.

LOOKING FORWARD

Bills of lading stand at a crossroads. Electronic documentation promises to solve age-old problems like late arrival of documents, but raises new questions about legal recognition and security. Blockchain technology offers innovative solutions, but requires legal frameworks to realise its potential. Autonomous vessels will challenge assumptions embedded in rules drafted for crewed ships. Climate change affects shipping routes and practices. Geopolitical tensions reshape trade patterns.

Throughout these changes, the essential functions of bills of lading—receipting cargo, evidencing contracts, and serving as documents of title—will remain necessary. The form may evolve from paper to pixels, but the purposes endure because they serve fundamental commercial needs. Australian law must adapt to enable beneficial innovation while maintaining the legal certainty that makes bills of lading work.

This book seeks to explain the current law, efficiently while examining future developments. My hope is that it serves present practitioners while preparing future ones for the evolving landscape of maritime commerce. If it makes bills of lading more comprehensible to some readers, enables better practice by others, and contributes to ongoing development of this important field, and refreshes my memory, it will have succeeded in its purpose.

John Gates
Brisbane
April, 2026

Chapter 1: Introduction to Bills of Lading

1.1 Historical Development and Evolution

The bill of lading has a rich history spanning several centuries, evolving from simple receipts into sophisticated legal instruments that underpin international trade. The earliest forms of bills of lading can be traced to Mediterranean trade in the medieval period, where merchants required written evidence of shipments entrusted to sea carriers.

During the sixteenth and seventeenth centuries, as maritime trade expanded, the bill of lading began to assume greater legal significance. English courts gradually recognised the document not merely as a receipt but as evidence of the contract of carriage and, crucially, as a document of title that could be transferred to represent ownership of the goods in transit. This development was essential for the growth of international commerce, as it allowed merchants to sell goods while they were still at sea, with the bill of lading serving as the key to obtaining delivery.

The Industrial Revolution and the advent of steamships in the nineteenth century brought new challenges. Carriers began to insert extensive exemption clauses into bills of lading to protect themselves from liability, leading to what became known as the "battle of the forms." This practice prompted calls for reform and standardisation, ultimately leading to international efforts to regulate the rights and obligations evidenced by bills of lading.

1.2 Definition and Nature of Bills of Lading

A bill of lading is a transport document issued by or on behalf of a carrier to a shipper, acknowledging that specified goods have been received on board a vessel or for shipment. At its core, the bill of lading serves three primary functions: it acts as a receipt for the goods shipped, provides evidence of the contract of carriage, and operates as a document of title to the goods.

The Carriage of Goods by Sea Act 1991 (Cth) provides the primary legislative framework in Australia for bills of lading, implementing the Hague-Visby Rules through its Schedule 1A. Section 11 of the Act defines a sea carriage document (which includes bills of lading) as "a document which is or contains evidence of a contract of carriage by sea and the taking over or loading of goods by the carrier, and by which the carrier undertakes to deliver the goods against surrender of the document." This definition is consistent with similar provisions in other common law jurisdictions, including the UK's Carriage of Goods by Sea Act 1992.

The unique characteristic that distinguishes the bill of lading from other transport documents is its quality as a document of title. This means that the lawful holder of the bill can demand delivery of the goods from the carrier, transfer rights in the goods by endorsing and delivering the bill and pledge the goods as security while they remain in transit. These features make the bill of lading indispensable in international sales, banking, and insurance operations.

1.3 The Bill of Lading in Modern Shipping Practice

In contemporary maritime commerce, the bill of lading remains the primary document governing the relationship between cargo interests and carriers, despite the emergence of alternative transport documents such as sea waybills and delivery orders. Its continued dominance reflects the commercial need for a negotiable document in letter of credit transactions and commodity trading.

Modern shipping practice involves various parties in the bill of lading transaction. The shipper or consignor is typically the party who contracts with the carrier for the transportation of goods. The carrier, usually a shipping line, issues the bill of lading and undertakes to carry the goods to the destination. The consignee is the party to whom the goods are to be delivered, which may be the shipper, the buyer of the goods, or a bank holding the bill as security.

Containerisation has fundamentally transformed the practical operation of bills of lading. Goods are now typically packed in containers at inland locations, sealed, and transported to the port. This has created challenges regarding the carrier's ability to verify the contents of containers and has led to the widespread use of "shipper's load and count" clauses, which limit the carrier's responsibility for statements about the goods in the bill.

The timing of bill of lading issuance has also assumed commercial importance. In letter of credit transactions, banks typically require a "shipped" bill of lading as proof that goods have actually been loaded on board the vessel. However, in modern practice, there may be a significant time lag between when containers are received at the terminal and when they are loaded on the vessel, creating practical difficulties for shippers who need documents quickly.

1.4 Overview of International Conventions

The international regulation of bills of lading has been characterised by successive attempts to achieve uniformity through multilateral conventions. These instruments seek to balance the interests of cargo owners, who desire comprehensive carrier liability, and shipowners, who seek protection from unlimited exposure to claims.

1.4.1 The Hague Rules (1924)

The International Convention for the Unification of Certain Rules of Law relating to Bills of Lading, adopted in Brussels in 1924 and commonly known as the Hague Rules, represented the first successful effort at international standardisation. The Rules were a compromise between carrier and cargo interests, establishing a minimum level of carrier responsibility while permitting certain defences and limitations.

Australia was not an original signatory to the Hague Rules, but implemented them through imperial legislation. The Sea-Carriage of Goods Act 1924 (Cth) gave the Hague Rules the force of law in Australia, applying them to outward shipments from Australian ports. The Rules mandate that carriers must properly and carefully load, handle, stow, carry, keep, care for, and discharge goods carried. They establish a catalogue of exceptions to liability, including perils of the sea, acts of God, acts of war, and inherent vice of the goods. Importantly, the Rules prohibit carriers from contracting out of their basic obligations, rendering clauses that reduce carrier liability below the prescribed standard null and void.

The limitation of liability provisions in the original Hague Rules allowed carriers to limit their liability to Â£100 per package or unit, a figure that quickly became outdated due to inflation and changes in cargo values.

1.4.2 The Hague-Visby Rules (1968/1979)

Recognition of the deficiencies in the Hague Rules led to the adoption of a Protocol in 1968, which amended the original convention. These amendments, known as the Hague-Visby Rules, came into force internationally in 1977. A further Protocol in 1979 introduced additional provisions related to the Special Drawing Right as the unit of account for limitation purposes.

Australia adopted the Hague-Visby Rules through the Carriage of Goods by Sea Act 1991 (Cth), which repealed the 1924 Act and gave effect to both the 1968 and 1979 Protocols. The Act applies the Hague-Visby Rules to both outward shipments from Australia and, importantly, to inward shipments to Australia, providing comprehensive coverage. The Rules are set out in Schedule 1A to the Act (as amended by the 1979 Protocol) and Schedule 1 (the unamended version).

The Hague-Visby Rules retained the basic structure of the Hague Rules but made several significant modifications. The financial limits for liability were substantially increased and expressed in terms of Special Drawing Rights (SDRs) or their equivalent, providing a more stable basis for limitation. Under Article IV rule 5 of the Hague-Visby Rules as implemented in Australia, the limitation is 666.67 units of account (SDRs) per package or unit, or 2 units of account per kilogram of gross weight of the goods lost or damaged, whichever is higher.

The amended Rules also extended coverage to circumstances where containers or pallets are used, addressing the modern reality of containerised shipping. Article IV rule 5(c) provides that where a container, pallet or similar article of transport is used to consolidate goods, the packages or shipping units enumerated in the bill of lading as packed in such article are deemed packages or units. This provision has been the subject of Australian case law interpreting what constitutes a "package" for limitation purposes.

Another important change introduced by the Hague-Visby Rules was the extension of the carrier's period of responsibility, which now runs from the time goods are loaded until they are discharged from the vessel. The Rules also introduced provisions dealing with the carrier's obligation regarding deck cargo and live animals, and clarified the position regarding delay in delivery.

1.4.3 The Hamburg Rules (1978)

Dissatisfaction with the carrier-friendly provisions of the Hague and Hague-Visby Rules, particularly among developing nations, led to the adoption of the United Nations Convention on the Carriage of Goods by Sea in Hamburg in

1978. The Hamburg Rules represent a significant departure from earlier conventions, substantially increasing carrier liability and reducing available defences.

Under the Hamburg Rules, the carrier is liable for loss, damage, or delay unless it can prove that it and its servants and agents took all measures that could reasonably be required to avoid the event and its consequences. This represents a reversal of the burden of proof compared to the Hague-Visby regime. The catalogue of excepted perils was abolished, and the carrier must affirmatively establish that it was not at fault.

The Hamburg Rules also extended the carrier's period of responsibility to cover the entire period during which the carrier is in charge of the goods, including the periods before loading and after discharge. Limitation amounts were increased, and the Rules introduced liability for delay in delivery, which had not been explicitly addressed in earlier conventions.

Australia has not ratified or implemented the Hamburg Rules, maintaining its commitment to the Hague-Visby regime. Despite the shipper-friendly provisions of the Hamburg Rules, they have not achieved widespread acceptance. Major maritime nations, including the United Kingdom, the United States, and most European countries have also not ratified the convention. This limited adoption has prevented the Hamburg Rules from achieving their goal of creating a uniform international regime.

1.4.4 The Rotterdam Rules (2009)

The most recent attempt at international harmonisation is the United Nations Convention on Contracts for the International Carriage of Goods Wholly or Partly by Sea, adopted in Rotterdam in 2009. These Rules represent an ambitious effort to create a modern, comprehensive regime that addresses multimodal transport and electronic commerce while balancing the interests of all stakeholders.

The Rotterdam Rules introduce several innovations. They apply to door-to-door carriage rather than only port-to-port, recognising the reality of modern container transport. They provide a detailed framework for electronic transport records, acknowledging the commercial pressure to replace paper documents with electronic alternatives. The liability regime attempts to strike a new balance between the Hague-Visby and Hamburg approaches, with a modified burden of proof and updated limitation amounts.

Significantly, the Rotterdam Rules address the role of maritime performing parties, including terminal operators and stevedores, providing them with the benefit of defences and limitations available to the carrier. They also introduce comprehensive provisions on delivery, including detailed rules for situations where no negotiable transport document has been issued or where goods arrive before documents.

Australia has not ratified the Rotterdam Rules and has indicated no immediate intention to do so. The Australian Government conducted consultations on the Rotterdam Rules but determined that the benefits of change did not outweigh the advantages of maintaining the well-established Hague-Visby framework. Like the Hamburg Rules, the Rotterdam Rules have not yet achieved the widespread ratification necessary to bring them into force internationally. As of 2026, only a handful of states have ratified the convention, and major maritime nations remain hesitant. The complexity of the Rules and disagreements about their provisions have slowed the ratification process.

1.5 Coexistence of Regimes

The failure of successive conventions to achieve universal acceptance has resulted in a fragmented international landscape where different regimes apply depending on the jurisdiction and the terms of the contract of carriage. This lack of uniformity creates complexity for parties engaged in international trade, who must navigate different liability rules, limitation amounts, and procedural requirements depending on which convention applies.

The applicable regime is typically determined by several factors: the law of the jurisdiction where suit is brought, the place of shipment or discharge, and the terms incorporated into the bill of lading itself. Many bills of lading contain "paramount clauses" that expressly incorporate one of the international conventions. Courts must then determine whether such incorporation is effective and which version of the rules applies when there is ambiguity.

This complexity underscores the continued importance of the bill of lading as a contractual document. While international conventions provide a baseline of mandatory rules, the specific terms of the bill of lading remain crucial in determining the parties' rights and obligations. Understanding both the applicable international framework and the particular terms of the transport document is essential for anyone involved in maritime commerce.

1.6 Conclusion

The bill of lading stands at the intersection of commerce and law, serving vital functions that enable international trade. Its evolution from a simple receipt to a sophisticated legal instrument reflects the development of maritime commerce itself. While international conventions have sought to create uniform rules, the persistence of multiple regimes demonstrates the difficulty of balancing the diverse interests involved in carriage by sea.

As we proceed through subsequent chapters, we will examine in detail the various functions of the bill of lading, the different types and forms it may take, and the legal principles governing its operation. Understanding these fundamentals is essential for grasping the complexities of modern shipping law and the continuing role of this venerable document in facilitating global trade.

Chapter 2: Functions of the Bill of Lading

2.1 Introduction

The bill of lading is unique among commercial documents in performing multiple, interconnected functions simultaneously. This multifunctional character gives the bill of lading its central importance in international trade but also creates potential complexities when the different functions come into conflict. This chapter examines each of the three primary functions "receipt, evidence of contract, and document of title" and explores how they interact in practice.

2.2 The Bill of Lading as a Receipt for Goods Shipped

2.2.1 Basic Function as Receipt

The most straightforward function of the bill of lading is to serve as a receipt, acknowledging that the carrier has received goods for shipment. This receipt function existed from the earliest days of maritime commerce and remains fundamental. When goods are delivered to the carrier, the bill of lading provides written confirmation of what has been received, including details about the quantity, description, apparent condition, and any identifying marks or numbers.

The receipt function serves several important purposes. For the shipper, it provides evidence that goods have been handed over to the carrier, which may be necessary to fulfill obligations under a sale contract. For the carrier, the bill documents what has been received, protecting against claims that goods were not delivered or were delivered in a different condition. For third parties, particularly banks financing the transaction, the bill provides assurance that goods actually exist and have been shipped.

2.2.2 Types of Statements in the Receipt

The statements contained in a bill of lading as a receipt typically include several categories of information. The quantity of goods is usually specified by number of packages, weight, volume, or other appropriate measure. The description identifies the nature of the goods, though the level of detail varies considerably depending on trade practice and the carrier's knowledge. The apparent order and condition notes any visible defects, damage, or irregularities observed when goods were received.

Leading marks and numbers are also recorded, identifying specific packages or shipments. These marks are particularly important in break-bulk cargo operations where multiple shippers' goods may be carried together. In containerised shipping, the container number serves a similar identifying function, though the carrier typically has no knowledge of the contents within sealed containers.

2.2.3 "Shipped" versus "Received for Shipment"

An important distinction exists between a "shipped" bill of lading and a "received for shipment" bill. A shipped bill of lading (also called an "on board" bill) certifies that goods have actually been loaded on board the named vessel. This provides greater assurance to the buyer and is typically required in letter of credit transactions. In contrast, a received for shipment bill merely acknowledges that the carrier has received the goods, which may still be at the terminal or warehouse awaiting loading.

The distinction became particularly significant with the development of container shipping, where goods might be received at a container yard weeks before actual vessel loading. To accommodate commercial demands for earlier documentation, carriers developed the practice of issuing received for shipment bills that could later be exchanged for shipped bills once loading occurred, or receiving for shipment bills that were subsequently stamped with an "on board" notation.

2.2.4 Limitations on the Receipt Function

The carrier's responsibility regarding statements in the bill of lading is not unlimited. The carrier can only be expected to acknowledge the apparent condition of goods, not their actual condition when concealed from view. This is particularly relevant with containerised cargo, where carriers routinely accept sealed containers without inspecting contents. Bills of lading for such shipments typically contain clauses such as "shipper's load, stow and count" or "said to contain," which qualify the carrier's statements and indicate that information comes from the shipper rather than the carrier's own knowledge.

These qualifying clauses have important legal consequences. They may limit the evidential value of statements in the bill and affect the carrier's liability for misstatements. However, such clauses cannot protect carriers from all responsibility. If the carrier knows or has reason to know that statements are incorrect, qualification clauses may not be effective. The legal effect of these qualifications is explored more fully in Chapter 5.

2.3 The Bill of Lading as Evidence of the Contract of Carriage

2.3.1 Evidential Function

The second major function of the bill of lading is to provide evidence of the contract of carriage. It is important to note that the bill itself is not typically the contract of carriage, particularly in liner shipping. The contract is usually concluded earlier, when the shipper books space on the vessel or delivers goods to the carrier. The bill of lading is then issued, recording the terms on which carriage has been undertaken.

This evidential function means the bill sets out the rights and obligations of carrier and cargo owner. The face of the bill identifies the parties, the goods, the voyage, and the freight payable. The reverse side (or sometimes a separate document incorporated by reference) contains the detailed terms and conditions governing the carriage. These terms address matters such as the carrier's obligations and exceptions, limitation of liability, jurisdiction, and procedures for making claims.

2.3.2 Contract Terms and Incorporation

The terms of carriage may be lengthy and detailed, covering numerous contingencies that might arise during the voyage. In liner shipping, these terms are typically standardised for all shipments on that shipping line. Many carriers use forms based on industry models, though terms may vary between carriers and trades.

A critical issue is whether and how terms are incorporated into the contract. Generally, terms printed on the bill of lading itself or on its reverse side are considered part of the contract. Terms contained in separate documents may also be incorporated if there is adequate reference to them in the bill. The requirement for incorporation is particularly important where a bill of lading incorporates terms from a charterparty, a matter addressed in Chapter 6.

2.3.3 The Bill in the Hands of the Original Shipper

As between the original shipper and the carrier, the bill of lading is merely evidence of the contract terms, not the contract itself. This means that if there is other evidence of what was actually agreed, that evidence may prevail over the terms stated in the bill. For example, if negotiations or correspondence between shipper and carrier established particular terms, those terms may govern even if the bill of lading states different terms.

This principle was recognised in Australian law in cases such as *SS Ardennes (Cargo Owners) v SS Ardennes (Owners)* [1951] 1 KB 55, which although a UK decision has been followed in Australia. The shipper, having been party to the original contract, cannot be prejudiced by statements in a document issued unilaterally by the carrier. The shipper may therefore introduce parol evidence to contradict or supplement the terms in the bill. However, this ability to look beyond the bill is limited to the original contracting parties and does not extend to third parties who later acquire the bill.

2.3.4 The Bill in the Hands of Third Parties

The position changes significantly when the bill of lading is transferred to a third party, such as a buyer of the goods. The third party was not present when the original contract was made and has no knowledge of what might have been agreed beyond what appears in the bill itself. For the third party, therefore, the bill of lading is not merely evidence of the contract but becomes the contract itself.

This rule is essential to the negotiability of bills of lading. A buyer receiving a bill in a chain of sales must be able to rely on the terms stated in the bill without investigating whether other terms might have been agreed between the original shipper and carrier. The bill becomes a self-contained statement of the contractual relationship between the carrier and the holder.

Courts have consistently held that third parties take the bill on its face and are bound by its terms, whether or not they have read those terms. This includes both the terms favourable to cargo interests and those favourable to the carrier. Onerous terms may be binding on a third-party holder even if the original shipper was unaware of them or did not specifically agree to them.

2.3.5 Conflict Between Receipt and Contract Functions

The dual function of the bill as both receipt and contract evidence can create tensions. Statements made in the bill as a receipt (regarding quantity, condition, etc.) may conflict with terms in the bill as a contract (such as exemption clauses). For example, the bill might state on its face that goods were received in good condition, while terms on the reverse exempt the carrier from liability for certain types of damage.

Generally, the receipt function prevails regarding statements of fact about the goods shipped, while the contract function prevails regarding the terms governing the carriage. However, the interplay can be complex, particularly where carriers have inserted qualification clauses that attempt to limit the receipt function. The resolution of such conflicts often depends on the specific wording used and the jurisdiction hearing the dispute.

2.4 The Bill of Lading as a Document of Title

2.4.1 The Concept of Document of Title

The most distinctive and commercially important function of the bill of lading is its character as a document of title to the goods. This means that possession of the bill, properly transferred, gives the holder the right to possession of the goods themselves. The bill represents the goods while they are in transit, allowing dealings with the goods through dealings with the document.

The concept of a document of title is an exception to the general common law principle that ownership of goods cannot be transferred by mere delivery of a document. This exception developed through mercantile custom and was recognised by courts as essential to maritime trade. By the nineteenth century, it was firmly established that a bill of lading could be endorsed and transferred, passing constructive possession and, in appropriate circumstances, ownership of the goods.

2.4.2 Transfer of Possession Through the Bill

The document of title function operates primarily at the level of possession rather than ownership. Possession of the bill gives the holder the right to claim physical possession of the goods from the carrier upon arrival at the destination. The carrier is obliged to deliver the goods only to the person who presents the bill of lading, properly endorsed if necessary.

This creates a form of "constructive possession" of the goods. While the goods are physically in the carrier's custody, legal possession is held by whoever has the bill. When the bill is transferred, possession of the goods is deemed to pass to the new holder even though the goods remain on the ship. This constructive possession is recognised for various legal purposes, including determining who has the right to sue for damage to goods and who bears the risk of loss.

2.4.3 Transfer of Property Through the Bill

While the document of title function primarily concerns possession, the bill of lading also plays a role in transferring ownership (property) in the goods. Under the Sale of Goods Act and commercial law principles, the intention of parties determines when property passes in a sale. In international sales, particularly CIF (Cost, Insurance, Freight) contracts, it is common for property to pass when the seller tenders shipping documents, including the bill of lading, to the buyer.

The transfer of the bill in such circumstances symbolises transfer of the goods themselves. The buyer, receiving the bill while goods are at sea, becomes owner of the goods even though physical delivery is still to occur. This mechanism allows goods to be sold multiple times while in transit, with each successive buyer taking ownership by receiving transfer of the bill of lading.

However, the relationship between transfer of the bill and transfer of property is not automatic. The bill facilitates transfer of ownership but does not itself vest property. The actual passing of property depends on the intention of the parties to the sale, as ascertained from their contract and conduct. The bill is the instrument through which that intention is effectuated, but the intention itself derives from the sale contract.

2.4.4 Rights of Suit and Statutory Intervention

Historically, a problem arose because common law did not automatically transfer contractual rights when the bill of lading was transferred. A buyer receiving the bill obtained the right to possession but not necessarily the right to sue the carrier for breach of the contract of carriage or for damage to goods.

This created a "legal black hole" where neither the original shipper (who no longer had property) nor the transferee (who had property but no contract) could sue.

This unsatisfactory situation was first addressed in the UK by the Bills of Lading Act 1855, which influenced Australian law. In Australia, the position is now governed by section 11 of the Carriage of Goods by Sea Act 1991 (Cth), which provides that the lawful holder of a bill of lading has transferred to and vested in them all rights of suit under the contract of carriage as if they had been a party to that contract. This provision is based on the UK's Carriage of Goods by Sea Act 1992 and represents a more refined approach than the earlier legislation.

Section 11(2) defines a "lawful holder" as a person in possession of the bill who, in good faith, has become the holder either by virtue of being the person to whom delivery was to be made according to the bill, or through having become the holder through transfer of the bill. The section also provides that rights are transferred when the person becomes the holder, or when the goods are delivered to the person pursuant to the bill, whichever occurs first.

These statutory provisions recognise that the document of title function requires not just physical possession rights but also contractual rights. A holder who can demand delivery of goods must also be able to sue if the goods are damaged or if the carrier breaches the contract. The legislative framework creates the necessary link between possession of the document and enforceability of the contract, adapting the common law to commercial reality.

2.4.5 Commercial Significance in Trade and Finance

The document of title function makes the bill of lading indispensable in several commercial contexts. In international sales, particularly commodity trades, goods are routinely sold multiple times during transit. Each buyer takes by receiving transfer of the bill, knowing that they can obtain delivery upon arrival. This "string trading" would be impossible without a negotiable document representing the goods.

In banking and trade finance, the bill of lading serves as security. Banks providing finance against documentary credits require bills of lading as collateral. If the buyer defaults, the bank holding the bill can obtain delivery of the goods and sell them to recover the debt. This security function depends entirely on the bill's character as a document of title.â€"a mere receipt or contract evidence would not provide equivalent protection.

The bill also facilitates insurance of goods in transit. Marine cargo insurance policies typically require the insured to have an insurable interest in the goods, which may be established through possession of the bill of lading. Insurance claims are also often assigned with the bill, allowing the buyer to recover insurance proceeds for damage occurring before they acquired ownership.

2.4.6 Limitations on Document of Title Status

Not all transport documents are documents of title, even if they evidence a contract of carriage. Sea waybills, for example, serve as receipts and evidence of contract but are not documents of title because they are not transferable and the carrier can deliver without their surrender. Straight bills of lading (non-negotiable bills consigned to a named consignee) have an uncertain status in many jurisdictions, with debate about whether they are true documents of title.

Even with negotiable bills of lading, the document of title function has limitations. The bill represents rights against the carrier and rights to delivery of goods, but it does not guarantee that those rights are valuable. If goods have been lost or destroyed, the bill may still be transferred, but the holder receives only the right to sue for loss, not the goods themselves. Similarly, if the carrier has become insolvent, the bill's value as security is diminished.

2.5 Interrelationship Between the Functions

2.5.1 Complementary Nature

The three functions of the bill of lading are not independent but interconnected. The receipt function provides the factual foundation, what goods were shipped and in what condition. The contract evidence function establishes the legal framework on what terms the goods are being carried. The document of title function enables commerce, allowing the goods to be traded and financed while in transit.

These functions support each other in practice. A buyer accepting transfer of a bill of lading relies on the receipt statements to know what goods they are buying, on the contract terms to understand their rights against the carrier, and on the document of title character to secure delivery. The removal of any one function would substantially diminish the utility of the others.

2.5.2 Potential Conflicts

Despite their complementary nature, the different functions can sometimes conflict. A common tension arises between the receipt function, where precision and accuracy are important, and the document of title function, which requires certainty and marketability. If bills contained numerous qualifications and caveats to ensure accuracy, they would be less readily transferable. Conversely, unqualified statements in bills might expose carriers to undue liability.

Another potential conflict exists between the contract function and the document of title function. Some terms that carriers wish to include (such as jurisdiction or arbitration clauses) may not be prominent on the face of the bill. Third parties taking the bill in good faith may be bound by terms they did not see and could not reasonably have been expected to investigate. Courts must balance the carrier's freedom of contract against the transferee's reasonable expectations.

2.5.3 Statutory and Judicial Reconciliation

Legal systems have developed various mechanisms to reconcile tensions between the functions. Statutory regimes like the Hague-Visby Rules prohibit certain terms that would undermine the receipt function or the basic obligations regarding care of goods, ensuring a minimum standard regardless of what the contract might say. Estoppel principles prevent carriers from denying the accuracy of statements in bills, protecting third parties who rely on those statements.

Courts also interpret bills of lading in ways that balance the functions. Ambiguous terms are often construed against the carrier who drafted them (contra proferentem). Receipt statements on the face of the bill are given greater weight than contradictory terms buried in fine print. These interpretive approaches help ensure that the bill of lading can effectively serve all its functions without one completely undermining another.

2.5.4 Evolution in Response to Commercial Needs

The relationship between the functions continues to evolve in response to changing commercial practices. Electronic bills of lading, now emerging, must replicate all three functions in a digital format, providing receipts, evidencing contracts, and conferring rights equivalent to possession of a physical document. This requires new technical and legal solutions to ensure that the essential functions are preserved.

Similarly, containerisation has affected how the functions operate. The receipt function is modified by the reality that carriers cannot inspect container contents. The document of title function must adapt to situations where containers are unpacked, and goods distributed before bills arrive. These developments demonstrate that the functions are not static but continually adapt to maintain relevance in changing commercial conditions.

2.6 Conclusion

The three functions of the bill of lading - receipt, evidence of contract, and document of title make it the most important document in maritime commerce. Each function serves distinct purposes, yet they are integrated into a single instrument that facilitates the complex operations of international trade. Understanding these functions and their interrelationship is essential for comprehending how bills of lading operate in practice and how legal principles governing them have developed.

The receipt function provides the factual record necessary for commercial dealings. The contract evidence function establishes the legal rights and obligations between carrier and cargo interests. The document of title function enables the negotiability and financing essential to international trade. Together, these functions explain why, despite technological changes and the emergence of alternative documents, the bill of lading remains central to shipping law and practice.

As we examine specific aspects of bills of lading in subsequent chapters, we will see how these functions manifest in different contexts in the various types of bills, in their issue and transfer, in disputes about their contents, and in the challenges of modern shipping. The functional analysis provided in this chapter provides the framework for understanding these more detailed considerations.

Chapter 3: Types and Forms of Bills of Lading

3.1 Introduction

Bills of lading exist in numerous forms, each developed to serve particular commercial needs and shipping practices. The choice of bill type has significant legal and commercial consequences, affecting the rights of parties, the negotiability of the document, and the applicable regulatory framework. This chapter examines the principal types and forms of bills of lading encountered in Australian and international trade, exploring their characteristics, uses, and legal implications.

Understanding the distinctions between different types of bills is essential for shipping practitioners, as the form selected determines crucial matters such as when risk passes, who may sue for cargo damage, and whether the document can serve as security for financing. The diversity of bill types reflects the adaptability of this ancient instrument to evolving commercial requirements.

3.2 Shipped versus Received for Shipment Bills

3.2.1 The Distinction

One of the fundamental distinctions in bills of lading relates to the timing of their issuance and what they certify about the status of the goods. A "shipped" bill of lading (also called an "on board" bill) certifies that goods have actually been loaded on board a named vessel. In contrast, a "received for shipment" bill acknowledges that the carrier has received the goods but does not confirm that loading has occurred.

The shipped bill provides greater certainty to buyers and financiers because it confirms that the goods are actually on their way to the destination. The bill will typically bear a notation such as "shipped on board" followed by the vessel name and the date of shipment. This represents the completion of the shipper's obligation to deliver goods to the carrier for transportation.

A received for shipment bill merely evidences that the carrier has taken custody of the goods, which may be in a warehouse, container yard, or terminal awaiting loading. The goods are under the carrier's control but have not yet commenced the sea voyage. This type of bill emerged to accommodate modern shipping practices where goods, particularly containerised cargo, may arrive at the port facility well before the vessel is ready for loading.

3.2.2 Commercial and Legal Significance

The distinction between shipped and received for shipment bills has important commercial implications, particularly in international sales and documentary credit transactions. Under the Uniform Customs and Practice for Documentary Credits (UCP 600), which governs most international letters of credit, banks typically require presentation of a shipped bill of lading unless the credit specifically permits a received for shipment bill.

This requirement reflects the buyer's and bank's preference for certainty that goods have actually commenced their voyage. A received for shipment bill creates uncertainty about when or even whether goods will be loaded. Goods might remain in the terminal for an extended period, be damaged while waiting, or even be loaded on a different vessel than originally intended.

Under Australian law and the Carriage of Goods by Sea Act 1991 (Cth), the carrier's responsibility under the Hague-Visby Rules begins when goods are loaded on board and ends when they are discharged. A received for shipment bill therefore evidences a period before the international convention rules apply, during which different terms may govern the carrier's liability. This can create complexity in determining what regime applies if goods are damaged while in the carrier's custody but not yet loaded.

3.2.3 Conversion and Notation Practices

To accommodate the commercial demand for shipped bills while dealing with the practical reality of early cargo reception, carriers developed the practice of issuing received for shipment bills that could later be converted to shipped bills. Once goods are loaded, the shipper may exchange the received for shipment bill for a shipped bill, or the carrier may add an "on board" notation to the original document.

The notation practice involves the carrier stamping or writing on the received for shipment bill a statement that goods have been shipped on board a named vessel, together with the date of shipment and an authorised signature. Article III rule 7 of the Hague-Visby Rules, as implemented in Australia, specifically recognises this practice, providing that where a received for shipment bill is issued, the carrier may add an on-board notation which, when signed, constitutes the date of shipment.

The date of the on-board notation becomes crucial for determining whether the shipper has complied with shipment deadlines under the sale contract. In documentary credits, banks will examine the on-board notation to verify timely shipment. Disputes sometimes arise about whether a notation is sufficient or whether it adequately identifies the vessel and shipment date.

3.3 Clean versus Claused Bills

3.3.1 Definition and Significance

A "clean" bill of lading is one that contains no notations, remarks, or clauses expressly stating that the goods or their packaging are defective or damaged. The bill acknowledges receipt of goods in apparent good order and condition without qualification. In contrast, a "claused" or "unclean" bill contains notations indicating some defect, damage, or irregularity in the goods or packaging as received.

The distinction is of critical importance in documentary credit transactions. Under UCP 600, banks must refuse documents that include a clause or notation indicating that goods or packaging are defective. Article 27 of UCP 600 specifically provides that a transport document must not indicate that the goods or their packaging are in defective condition. Only a clean bill of lading is acceptable under a letter of credit unless the credit specifically permits clausing.

This commercial requirement reflects the buyer's expectation of receiving goods in satisfactory condition. If the bill indicates damage or defects, the buyer is forewarned that the goods may not meet contractual specifications. Banks, acting as intermediaries in the payment process, refuse claused bills to protect the buyer's interests and to avoid involvement in disputes about the condition of goods.

3.3.2 Types of Clauses

Clauses appearing on bills of lading vary widely in their content and implications. Common examples include notations such as "one carton torn," "rusty drums," "packaging damaged," "second-hand cases," or "said to be leaking." Each such clause indicates that the carrier observed something irregular when goods were received.

Some clauses relate to the quantity of goods, such as "three packages missing" or "quantity not verified." Others concern the packaging, like "insufficiently packed" or "packaging unsuitable for sea voyage." Still others relate to the apparent condition of the goods themselves, though carriers can usually only comment on what is visible from outside sealed packages or containers.

The effect of clausing is to qualify the carrier's acknowledgment of receipt and to limit the carrier's liability. If the bill states that goods were received with damaged packaging, the carrier cannot later be held responsible for damage that might have resulted from that pre-existing condition. The clause serves as a reservation protecting the carrier from claims for conditions that existed when goods were received.

3.3.3 Letters of Indemnity

The commercial unacceptability of claused bills in letter of credit transactions creates pressure on shippers to obtain clean bills even when some defect or irregularity exists. This has led to the widespread but legally problematic practice of letters of indemnity. Under this arrangement, the shipper provides the carrier with a letter of indemnity (LOI) agreeing to indemnify the carrier against any liability arising from issuing a clean bill despite observed defects.

In exchange for the LOI, the carrier issues a clean bill without noting the defects. This allows the shipper to present complying documents to the bank and obtain payment. However, the practice is fraught with legal and ethical difficulties. The carrier is essentially making a false statement in the bill, which may constitute fraud, particularly when the bill is transferred to innocent third parties who rely on the clean statement.

Australian courts, following English authorities, have held that letters of indemnity cannot protect carriers who knowingly issue false bills of lading. In *Brown Jenkinson & Co Ltd v Percy Dalton (London) Ltd* [2 QB 621], followed in Australia, it was established that an agreement to indemnify a carrier for issuing a false bill is unenforceable as contrary to public policy. The carrier cannot recover under the LOI because it is based on an illegal contract.

Furthermore, issuing a clean bill when goods are known to be damaged may expose the carrier to criminal liability for fraud, particularly if third parties suffer loss by relying on the false statement. Article III rule 5 of the Hague-Visby Rules, as implemented in the Carriage of Goods by Sea Act 1991 (Cth), provides that the carrier shall be deemed to have guaranteed the accuracy of statements in the bill regarding marks, number, quantity, and apparent order and condition. Deliberately false statements breach this statutory duty.

Despite these legal risks, letters of indemnity remain common in practice, particularly where defects are minor and where the carrier has an ongoing commercial relationship with a trusted shipper. However, prudent carriers refuse to issue clean bills when significant defects exist, recognising that the short-term commercial benefit does not justify the legal exposure.

3.3.4 The Carrier's Duty to Clause

Carriers face a duty to accurately describe the apparent condition of goods received. This duty arises both from the contract of carriage and from the carrier's responsibility to third parties who may rely on statements in the bill. The carrier must exercise reasonable care in inspecting goods and noting any visible defects or irregularities.

However, the carrier's duty is limited to what can be reasonably observed. The carrier is not required to open sealed packages or containers to inspect contents. When receiving sealed containers packed by the shipper, carriers routinely qualify their statements with phrases such as "shipper's load, stow and count" or "said to contain," indicating that the description of contents comes from the shipper rather than the carrier's own observation.

The extent of inspection required depends on the circumstances. For break-bulk cargo visible to the carrier, more detailed inspection is expected. For containerised cargo delivered as sealed units, limited inspection is reasonable. Australian courts recognise these practical limitations while requiring that carriers exercise reasonable diligence regarding matters they can observe, such as the external condition of containers and the apparent condition of non-containerised cargo.

3.4 Straight, Order, and Bearer Bills

3.4.1 Order Bills (Negotiable Bills)

An order bill of lading is one that is transferable by endorsement and delivery, making it a fully negotiable document. The bill will typically be made out "to order" or "to the order of [named party]." This is the most common form of bill in international trade because it provides maximum flexibility for subsequent dealings with the goods while in transit.

An order bill can be transferred multiple times during the voyage through endorsement on the back of the bill and physical delivery to the new holder. Each transfer passes constructive possession of the goods and, depending on the intention of the parties, may also transfer ownership. This negotiability is essential for commodity trading where goods are often sold several times while at sea, with each buyer taking by receiving the endorsed bill.

Under Australian law, the negotiability of order bills is recognised both by common law and by statute. Section 11 of the Carriage of Goods by Sea Act 1991 (Cth) provides that the lawful holder of a bill of lading has rights of suit against the carrier, with "lawful holder" defined to include a person who has become holder through transfer of the bill. This statutory recognition ensures that transferees can enforce the contract of carriage.

The order bill may be made out in different forms: "to order" (meaning to the order of the shipper), "to the order of [named party]" (requiring that party's endorsement for transfer), or "to order of shipper" (expressly stating the shipper's control). Once endorsed in blank (signed without naming a transferee), the bill becomes transferable by delivery alone without further endorsement, though subsequent holders may add restrictive endorsements.

3.4.2 Straight Bills (Non-Negotiable Bills)

A straight bill of lading, also called a non-negotiable bill, is one that is consigned directly to a named consignee without the words "to order." The bill states simply "consigned to [named party]" or "deliver to [named party]." Unlike order bills, straight bills are not transferable by endorsement and are not documents of title in the full sense.

The carrier under a straight bill must deliver goods to the named consignee regardless of who presents the bill. The consignee's right to delivery does not depend on possession of the bill but on being the named party. This means the bill cannot be used to transfer ownership during transit, and the goods cannot be pledged as security by transferring the bill to a bank.

Straight bills are used when the shipper does not want the goods to be tradeable in transit or when rapid delivery is required without waiting for documents. They are common in shipments between related companies (parent to subsidiary), in trades where documents will not arrive before the vessel, and in some regional trades where negotiability is not needed.

The legal status of straight bills has been somewhat controversial. They clearly serve as receipts and evidence of the contract of carriage, but their character as documents of title is disputed. Some jurisdictions treat them as non-negotiable documents of title, while others deny them that status entirely. In Australia, the better view is that straight bills are not documents of title because possession of the document does not confer the right to delivery. Only being the named consignee does.

Section 11 of the Carriage of Goods by Sea Act 1991 (Cth) extends rights of suit to the consignee named in a non-negotiable bill, ensuring they can enforce the contract. However, the consignee takes those rights by virtue of being named, not by transfer of the document. This distinction is important because it means intermediate holders of a straight bill do not acquire rights merely by possessing the document.

3.4.3 Bearer Bills

A bearer bill is one that is made out "to bearer" without naming a consignee. The bill is transferable by delivery alone, without any endorsement. Whoever holds the bill in good faith is entitled to delivery of the goods. This makes bearer bills the most freely transferable form.

However, bearer bills are rare in modern practice because they present significant security risks. Loss or theft of a bearer bill means loss of the goods, as the carrier must deliver to whoever presents the document. Banks are reluctant to accept bearer bills because the risk of loss is high. Most trades and documentary credit transactions require order bills rather than bearer bills.

The Hague-Visby Rules, as implemented in Australia, apply to bearer bills just as to other forms. However, the practical risks associated with bearer bills mean they are generally avoided except in specialised circumstances where immediate transferability without endorsement formalities is essential.

3.4.4 Commercial Choice Between Forms

The choice between order, straight, and bearer bills depends on commercial circumstances. Order bills are preferred when:

- Goods may be sold during transit.
- The bill will be used as security for financing.
- Maximum flexibility is desired.
- Documentary credit terms require a negotiable bill.

Straight bills are appropriate when:
- Shipper and consignee are related parties.
- Speed of delivery is more important than negotiability.
- The trade does not involve letters of credit.
- The risk of documents arriving after the vessel is high.

Bearer bills are rare but might be used when:
- Immediate transferability is essential.
- Goods are being delivered to "bearer" by prior arrangement.
- Specialised trade practices require this form.

In practice, the vast majority of international shipments use order bills because they provide the flexibility essential to modern trade finance and commodity trading. Straight bills serve a niche role in particular trades, while bearer bills have largely disappeared from mainstream commerce.

3.5 Through Bills, Transhipment Bills, and Combined Transport Documents

3.5.1 Through Bills of Lading

A through bill of lading is issued for carriage that involves more than one leg or carrier, but where a single carrier takes responsibility for the entire journey. The bill covers the complete movement from origin to final destination, even though the actual carriage may be performed by different vessels or even different modes of transport.

For example, goods shipped from Melbourne to a final destination in Europe might require carriage to Singapore on one vessel and onward carriage on a different vessel to Rotterdam. A through bill issued by the first carrier covers the entire journey to Rotterdam, even though that carrier does not operate the second leg.

The through bill is convenient for shippers because they deal with a single carrier and a single contract for the entire journey. The issuing carrier becomes responsible for the full carriage, including segments performed by others. This contrasts with the shipper arranging separate contracts for each leg, which would require multiple bills and create complexity about where responsibility lies if goods are damaged.

Under Australian law and the Hague-Visby Rules, questions arise about whether the international convention applies to through bills, particularly for segments not involving sea carriage. Article X of the Hague-Visby Rules addresses this, stating that the Rules apply to bills of lading covering carriage from one port to another in different states, but permits carriers to incorporate in the bill terms applying to inland carriage segments.

The issuing carrier of a through bill typically incorporates terms specifying that responsibility for different segments may be governed by different liability regimes. For the sea portion, the Hague-Visby Rules apply as implemented by the Carriage of Goods by Sea Act 1991 (Cth). For inland portions, different terms may apply, such as those governing road or rail carriage. The bill may also contain "Himalaya clauses" extending protections to sub-contractors performing parts of the carriage.

3.5.2 Transhipment Bills

A transhipment bill specifically acknowledges that goods will be transferred from one vessel to another during the voyage to the final destination. The bill identifies both the initial carrying vessel and indicates that transhipment will occur at a specified port. This differs from a through bill where transhipment may occur but is not necessarily specified.

Transhipment introduces additional handling and risk, as goods must be unloaded, stored temporarily, and reloaded. Documentary credit practice generally disfavours transhipment unless expressly permitted in the credit terms. Under UCP 600, transhipment is prohibited unless the credit permits it or unless it is evidenced by a transport document covering the entire journey under a single contract.

Where transhipment occurs, questions may arise about carrier liability if goods are damaged during the transhipment process. The Hague-Visby Rules apply only while goods are loaded on the vessel, so periods between vessels at the transhipment port may fall outside the convention regime. Carriers typically include specific terms in bills of lading addressing liability during transhipment, often limiting responsibility or requiring the cargo owner to claim against the particular vessel or sub-carrier responsible.

3.5.3 Combined Transport Documents and Multimodal Bills

Combined transport documents (also called multimodal or intermodal transport documents) cover carriage by more than one mode of transport, such as sea, rail, road, or air. These documents emerged with containerisation, which enables seamless movement of cargo across different transport modes without unpacking.

A combined transport bill might cover, for example, carriage from an inland depot in Australia by truck to the port, ocean carriage to a foreign port, and onward rail carriage to an inland destination. The issuing carrier (called a multimodal transport operator or MTO) takes responsibility for the entire door-to-door movement.

The legal framework for combined transport documents is complex because different conventions govern different modes. The Hague-Visby Rules apply only to sea carriage. Road transport may be governed by the CMR Convention, rail by CIM, and air by the Warsaw or Montreal Conventions. The multimodal transport operator must navigate these different regimes in drafting the bill of lading terms.

Australia has not adopted the UN Convention on International Multimodal Transport of Goods, and there is no specific Australian statute governing multimodal transport. The Carriage of Goods by Sea Act 1991 (Cth) applies to the sea leg of a multimodal journey, but other segments are governed by the applicable mode-specific conventions or domestic law. This creates potential uncertainty about liability standards for different portions of the journey.

Multimodal transport operators typically address this uncertainty by incorporating the UNCTAD/ICC Rules for Multimodal Transport Documents or similar industry standards into their bills of lading. These rules provide a comprehensive framework for multimodal carriage, including a network liability system where the applicable liability regime depends on where in the journey damage occurred.

3.5.4 House Bills and Master Bills

In consolidated container shipping, a distinction exists between house bills and master bills. A master bill of lading is issued by the ocean carrier to a freight forwarder or consolidator who has arranged to ship containers containing cargo from multiple shippers. The freight forwarder then issues individual house bills of lading to each shipper whose cargo is in the container.

From the perspective of the individual shipper, the house bill is their contract with the freight forwarder. It serves as their receipt, evidence of their contract, and (if negotiable) their document of title. However, the actual ocean carrier has issued only the master bill to the forwarder and may have no contractual relationship with the individual shippers.

This creates potential complications for the ultimate cargo owner. If goods are damaged, the cargo owner's direct contractual relationship is with the freight forwarder (under the house bill) not the ocean carrier (under the master bill). The freight forwarder may have limited liability or may become insolvent, leaving the cargo owner unable to recover. Conversely, the ocean carrier may not recognise the holder of a house bill as having rights under the master bill.

To address these issues, some house bills contain terms making the forwarder the agent of the cargo owner for the purpose of contracting with the carrier, attempting to create direct contractual rights between cargo owner and carrier. The effectiveness of such terms is uncertain and may depend on whether the carrier was aware of and agreed to the agency arrangement. The legal position of house bill holders remains an area of some uncertainty in Australian shipping law.

3.6 Specialised Forms of Bills of Lading

3.6.1 Charter Party Bills of Lading

When a vessel is chartered, bills of lading may be issued either by the shipowner or by the charterer depending on the type of charter. Under a voyage charter, the shipowner typically remains responsible for cargo and issues bills of lading. Under a demise (bareboat) charter, the charterer takes full control and may issue bills. Under a time charter, either party may issue bills depending on the arrangements.

Charter party bills of lading raise special issues because the charter party contract and the bill of lading are separate documents that may contain different terms. The charter party is the agreement between shipowner and charterer for hire of the vessel. Bills of lading are issued for individual cargo shipments, often to third parties who are not parties to the charter party.

To avoid inconsistency, charter party bills typically contain incorporation clauses attempting to incorporate the terms of the charter party into the bill of lading contract. A typical clause might state "all terms, conditions, liberties and exceptions of the charter party dated [date] are incorporated herein." This raises questions about which charter party terms are effectively incorporated and how conflicts between charter party and bill of lading terms are resolved, issues addressed in detail in Chapter 6.

Under Australian law, charter party bills are subject to the Carriage of Goods by Sea Act 1991 (Cth) and the Hague-Visby Rules like any other bill, with some qualifications. Section 9(2) of the Act provides that the Rules do not apply to charterparties, but section 9(3) clarifies that the Rules do apply to bills of lading issued under a charterparty from the moment such bill regulates relations between carrier and a holder who is not the charterer.

This means that while the charter party itself is not governed by the Hague-Visby Rules, bills issued under the charter party are governed by the Rules when transferred to third parties. The charterer dealing directly with the shipowner under the charter party does not get the benefit of the Rules, but a bill of lading holder who is not the charterer does. This distinction reflects the policy of protecting third parties who take bills without knowledge of the charter party terms.

3.6.2 Groupage or Consolidation Bills

Groupage bills (also called consolidation bills) are issued by freight forwarders who consolidate cargo from multiple shippers into a single container or shipment. These are similar to house bills in that the forwarder issues bills to individual shippers while the ocean carrier issues a master bill to the forwarder.

The groupage bill serves the shipper's need for a bill of lading while enabling the economies of consolidation. Small shippers who cannot fill a container can share space, with the forwarder handling the consolidation and de-consolidation. However, the legal relationships are complex, as the shipper's bill is with the forwarder (not the ocean carrier) and the shipper relies on the forwarder's creditworthiness and competence.

3.6.3 Container Bills

Modern shipping is dominated by containerisation, and most bills of lading today are container bills. These bills typically identify the container number and may include notations such as "shipper's load and count" or "said to contain," reflecting that the carrier has no knowledge of the container contents.

Container bills raise particular issues regarding what constitutes a "package" for limitation purposes under the Hague-Visby Rules. Article IV rule 5(c) addresses this, providing that where goods are consolidated in containers, the packages or units enumerated in the bill as packed in the container are deemed the packages for limitation purposes. This prevents carriers from claiming that the entire container is one package with a single limitation amount.

Australian courts have examined this provision in cases such as *El Greco (Australia) Pty Ltd v Mediterranean Shipping Co SA* [2004] FCA 202, which addressed what constitutes proper enumeration of packages in container bills. The case confirmed that to obtain the benefit of per-package limitation, the bill must clearly identify the number of packages within the container.

3.6.4 Shipped on Deck Bills

Bills of lading for cargo shipped on deck require special mention because deck carriage creates additional risks and may affect the carrier's rights and obligations. Deck cargo is exposed to greater risk from weather and sea and may be jettisoned in emergency situations to save the vessel.

Article I(c) of the Hague-Visby Rules defines "goods" as including goods carried on deck only where such carriage is in accordance with agreement or usage of trade. Article VII allows carriers and cargo to agree that goods may be carried on deck, but such carriage must be noted in the bill of lading.

Where deck carriage is properly noted and agreed, the Hague-Visby Rules apply with appropriate modifications. However, unauthorised deck carriage, where goods are carried on deck contrary to the contract or without disclosure in the bill, may constitute a fundamental breach depriving the carrier of the right to limit liability. Australian courts have followed English authorities in holding that unauthorised deck carriage may amount to deviation, disentitling the carrier from relying on limitation and exception clauses.

Bills for containerised cargo often contain clauses permitting deck carriage, reflecting the commercial reality that containers are routinely carried on deck. Such clauses, if adequately brought to the cargo owner's attention, are generally effective to authorise deck carriage.

3.6.5 Liner Bills and Tramp Bills

A general distinction can be drawn between liner bills and tramp bills, though this is more a matter of trade classification than strict legal differentiation. Liner bills are issued for cargo carried on regular liner services operating on fixed routes and schedules. These bills typically use standard forms with detailed printed terms on the reverse.

Liner bills are usually issued to multiple shippers for general cargo, with the carrier offering space to anyone wishing to ship. The terms are standardised and non-negotiable, reflecting the carrier's published tariff. Major liner operators may have their own standard bill forms, often based on industry models like the CONLINEBILL or similar.

Tramp bills, in contrast, are associated with tramp shipping where vessels do not operate on fixed routes but go wherever cargo is available. Tramp shipping often involves full cargo loads and may occur under charter parties. The bills are more individualised and may incorporate charter party terms.

From a legal perspective, both liner and tramp bills are subject to the same fundamental principles and statutory framework in Australia. The Carriage of Goods by Sea Act 1991 (Cth) applies to both. However, the practical operation differs because liner bills typically involve third-party consignees while tramp bills more often remain with the charterer.

3.7 Electronic Bills of Lading

3.7.1 The Need for Electronic Alternatives

Despite centuries of evolution, the traditional paper bill of lading has significant disadvantages in modern commerce. Paper documents can be lost, stolen, or delayed. They require physical handling and courier costs. Most critically, in containerised shipping, vessels often arrive at destination ports before the bills of lading, creating practical difficulties for obtaining delivery.

These inefficiencies have driven efforts to develop electronic bills of lading that replicate the functions of paper bills in digital form. An effective electronic bill must serve as a receipt, evidence the contract, and function as a document of title, all in electronic format. The third function presents the greatest challenge because it requires creating an electronic record that can be "possessed" and transferred in ways that replicate physical possession and transfer of paper.

3.7.2 Legal Recognition in Australia

Australian law has taken steps to accommodate electronic bills of lading, though gaps remain. The Electronic Transactions Act 1999 (Cth) provides general recognition of electronic transactions and establishes that legal requirements for writing can be satisfied by electronic communications if the information is accessible for subsequent reference.

However, the Electronic Transactions Act specifically excludes certain transactions from its application, including "a transaction relating to the creation, transfer or transmission of interests in real property" (Schedule 1). Whether this exclusion applies to bills of lading, which are documents of title to goods, has been debated. The better view is that the exclusion relates to land and does not prevent electronic bills of lading, but uncertainty remains.

More specifically for maritime commerce, section 11 of the Carriage of Goods by Sea Act 1991 (Cth) refers to "bills of lading" without specifying that they must be in paper form. The section defines rights of the "lawful holder," which could potentially include a person with control of an electronic record, though this requires interpretation beyond the plain language.

The Rotterdam Rules (not yet in force and not adopted by Australia) contain comprehensive provisions for electronic transport records in Chapter 3. These provisions establish the concept of "exclusive control" as the electronic equivalent of possession, and provide detailed rules for transfer of electronic records. If and when the Rotterdam Rules enter into force, they would provide a clear legal framework for electronic bills of lading in participating countries.

3.7.3 Electronic Systems in Practice

Several electronic systems have been developed to facilitate electronic bills of lading, each using different technological approaches. The Bolero system (Bill of Lading Electronic Registry Organisation), established in 1999, creates electronic bills through a central registry that maintains records of the current holder. Transfer occurs by updating the registry to show a new holder.

The essDOCS (ICE Digital Trade) system uses a similar registry model but with a focus on commodity trading. The title registry maintains a record of the holder, and transfer is affected by instructions to the registry. Both Bolero and essDOCS operate on the basis of multilateral contracts among users, ensuring that all participants recognise the electronic records as equivalent to paper bills.

More recently, blockchain-based solutions have emerged, using distributed ledger technology to create and transfer electronic bills without a central registry. These systems create unique digital tokens representing the bill of lading, with transfer occurring through blockchain transactions that change ownership of the token. The immutable and transparent nature of blockchain records provides security and prevents double-spending (multiple transfers of the same bill).

Examples of blockchain-based electronic bill systems include TradeLens (developed by Maersk and IBM), WAVE, CargoX, and others. These platforms aim to create an ecosystem where carriers, shippers, banks, and other parties can interact using verified digital credentials and transferable electronic bills.

3.7.4 Practical and Legal Challenges

Despite technological solutions, electronic bills face ongoing challenges. Legal uncertainty in many jurisdictions about whether electronic bills qualify as documents of title hampers adoption. Not all parties in the shipping chain may participate in a particular electronic system, requiring fallback to paper documents.

Banking practice remains conservative, with many banks preferring paper bills for documentary credits despite the theoretical acceptance of electronic records. Insurance practices also assume paper documentation, creating friction when attempting to use electronic alternatives.

The lack of an internationally recognised legal framework is a significant barrier. While individual electronic systems have contractual frameworks binding their users, third parties not part of those systems may not recognise the electronic records. This limits the transferability essential to the document of title function.

Nevertheless, electronic bills of lading represent the future direction of the industry. The COVID-19 pandemic accelerated digital transformation, and pressure continues to grow for paperless documentation. Industry organisations such as the International Chamber of Commerce and UNCITRAL continue to work on standards and model laws to facilitate electronic bills.

3.7.5 Australian Developments

In Australia, several initiatives have explored electronic bills of lading. The Australian shipping industry has participated in international electronic systems like Bolero. Port authorities and terminal operators have implemented electronic systems for receiving and processing cargo documentation, though these typically fall short of creating true electronic bills of lading with document of title characteristics.

Legislative reform may be necessary to provide full certainty for electronic bills of lading in Australia. This could involve amendments to the Carriage of Goods by Sea Act 1991 (Cth) to expressly recognise electronic bills and define the requirements for their creation and transfer. Alternatively, Australia might adopt provisions similar to those in the Rotterdam Rules if that convention gains broader international acceptance.

The Law Council of Australia and industry groups have advocated for legal reforms to facilitate electronic bills, but concrete legislative action has been limited. In the interim, parties using electronic bills in Australian trades rely on contractual arrangements and the general provisions of the Electronic Transactions Act, accepting some degree of legal uncertainty.

3.8 Sea Waybills and Other Non-Negotiable Documents

3.8.1 Sea Waybills

A sea waybill (also called an ocean waybill or express bill) is a transport document that serves as a receipt and evidence of the contract of carriage but is not a document of title. Unlike a bill of lading, a sea waybill is not transferable and does not need to be surrendered to obtain delivery of the goods.

The waybill names a consignee to whom the carrier must deliver the goods. Delivery is made on proof of identity - the carrier verifies that the person claiming goods is the named consignee and releases cargo without requiring presentation of any document. This eliminates the risk of goods arriving before documents and the associated costs and delays.

Sea waybills are increasingly used in trades where:

- The shipper and consignee are related parties (parent-subsidiary shipments)
- The voyage is short and documents would not arrive before the vessel.
- Negotiability is not needed (goods will not be sold in transit)
- Speed and simplicity are priorities.

The legal framework for sea waybills in Australia is somewhat less developed than for bills of lading. The Carriage of Goods by Sea Act 1991 (Cth) applies the Hague-Visby Rules to "contracts of carriage covered by a bill of lading or any similar document of title." Whether a sea waybill is a "similar document of title" is debatable given that waybills are not documents of title in the traditional sense.

However, section 11 of the Carriage of Goods by Sea Act 1991 (Cth) addresses "sea carriage documents" including non-negotiable documents. Subsection

11(6) provides that where a sea carriage document is not a bill of lading (such as a waybill), rights of suit are transferred to the person to whom delivery is to be made under the document. This ensures that consignees named in waybills can enforce the contract of carriage.

3.8.2 Delivery Orders

A delivery order is a document issued by a seller or holder of goods authorising a carrier or warehouseman to release goods to a specified person. While similar to bills of lading in some respects, delivery orders are not issued by carriers and do not serve the same functions.

In shipping practice, delivery orders may be issued when bulk cargo is split among multiple buyers, with each buyer receiving a delivery order for their portion. The carrier holds the master bill of lading but will release specific quantities against presentation of delivery orders.

Australian law recognises delivery orders in certain contexts. The Sale of Goods Act 1923 (NSW) and equivalent legislation in other states provide that an acknowledgment by the carrier that they hold goods on behalf of a specified person may be effective to pass property. However, delivery orders lack the negotiable character and document of title status of bills of lading.

3.8.3 Ship's Delivery Orders

Ship's delivery orders are issued by the ship or its agent when cargo is to be split among multiple consignees but only one bill of lading exists. Each consignee receives a delivery order for their share of the cargo. These are common in bulk commodity trades where large shipments are divided among buyers at the discharge port.

The legal effect of ship's delivery orders depends on whether they are recognised by the carrier and whether they create contractual rights. Generally, ship's delivery orders do not themselves create contracts of carriage but serve as authorities for the carrier to release specific portions of cargo.

3.9 Stale Bills of Lading

A "stale" bill of lading is one that is presented in a documentary credit transaction after the time limits specified in the credit or, in the absence of specific terms, beyond a reasonable time. Under UCP 600, transport documents must be presented within 21 days of shipment unless the credit specifies otherwise.

Stale bills create practical and legal difficulties. The goods may have already arrived at destination, making the document of title function moot. The carrier may have already delivered goods, potentially to someone other than the lawful holder of the bill. Banks refuse stale bills in documentary credits because they indicate a breakdown in the documentary chain.

From a legal perspective, a stale bill remains valid. And the rights it evidences do not expire merely because time has passed. However, if the carrier has delivered goods without requiring surrender of the bill (perhaps because the goods had been awaiting collection for an extended period), the holder of the stale bill may find they have only a claim for wrongful delivery rather than a right to the goods themselves.

3.10 Conclusion

The diversity of bill of lading types reflects the instrument's remarkable adaptability to different commercial needs. From shipped to received for shipment bills, from clean to claused, from negotiable to straight bills, each variant serves specific purposes in facilitating trade.

Understanding these distinctions is essential for anyone involved in international shipping. The type of bill determines crucial matters: whether goods can be sold in transit, whether the document is acceptable for documentary credits, what risks the parties bear, and who can enforce the contract of carriage. Choosing the wrong type of bill can have serious commercial and legal consequences.

As shipping practice continues to evolve, particularly with digitalisation, new forms of transport documentation emerge. Electronic bills of lading may eventually replace paper entirely, requiring legal systems to adapt traditional concepts of possession and negotiability to the digital realm. Yet despite technological change, the fundamental purposes served by bills of lading, ie receipting, contract evidence, and document of title remain constant.

The next chapters will examine how these various types of bills are issued and transferred, what they state about the goods, and how they function as evidence of the contract of carriage. The typology established in this chapter provides the foundation for understanding these operational aspects of bills of lading in practice.

Chapter 4: Issue and Transfer of Bills of Lading

4.1 Introduction

The issuance and transfer of bills of lading are critical moments in the life of these documents. Issue marks the creation of the legal instrument and the formal acknowledgment of the carrier's receipt of goods and undertaking to carry them. Transfer enables the document of title function, allowing goods to change hands while in transit and facilitating trade finance. This chapter examines the legal principles and practical considerations surrounding the issue and transfer of bills of lading under Australian law.

Understanding these processes is essential because rights and obligations flow from the proper issue and transfer of bills. An improperly issued bill may not bind the carrier or may not be enforceable by third parties. A defective transfer may fail to pass rights in the goods or the ability to sue for their loss. The formalities and legal consequences of issue and transfer must therefore be carefully observed.

4.2 Who May Issue a Bill of Lading

4.2.1 The Carrier as Issuer

The bill of lading is fundamentally a document issued by or on behalf of the carrier. The carrier, in issuing the bill, acknowledges receipt of goods and undertakes to carry them to the destination. Under section 11 of the Carriage of Goods by Sea Act 1991 (Cth), a bill of lading is defined as a document "by which the carrier undertakes to deliver the goods against surrender of the document."

The term "carrier" in this context means the party who contracts to carry goods by sea. This may be the shipowner who operates the vessel, but in modern liner shipping is more commonly a shipping line or carrier company that may not own the vessels it uses. The carrier issues the bill whether or not it is also the actual owner of the vessel performing the carriage.

In voyage charter situations, the shipowner typically remains the carrier and issues bills of lading. In time charter arrangements, the position is more complex. The time charterer may have authority under the charter party to issue bills of lading binding the shipowner, even though the charterer is not the owner. The master of the vessel, as agent for the shipowner, may also issue bills. The question of whose bills bind whom in charter party contexts involves consideration of agency principles and the specific terms of the charter.

4.2.2 Issue by Agents

Bills of lading are frequently issued by agents acting on behalf of the carrier rather than by the carrier directly. The master of the vessel is the traditional agent authorised to issue bills, and bills signed by the master bind the shipowner. The master's authority to issue bills derives from their position as commander of the vessel and general agent for the shipowner in matters relating to the voyage.

In modern practice, bills are more commonly issued by shore-based agents, including:

- The carrier's port agents
- Loading brokers
- Freight forwarders (when acting as carrier or as agent for carrier)
- NVOCC (Non-Vessel Operating Common Carrier) operators.

For a bill issued by an agent to bind the carrier, the agent must have actual or apparent authority to issue bills on the carrier's behalf. Actual authority may be express (granted by written agreement) or implied (arising from the agent's position or course of dealing). Apparent or ostensible authority exists where the carrier has held out the agent as having authority, leading third parties to reasonably believe the agent can bind the carrier.

The question of authority becomes critical when an unauthorised person issues a bill. If a person without authority issues a bill purporting to be from a carrier, the carrier may not be bound by that bill. However, if the carrier has represented that person as having authority, the carrier may be estopped from denying the validity of the bill as against innocent third parties who relied on the apparent authority.

Australian courts apply general agency principles in determining whether bills issued by agents bind carriers. In *Freeman & Lockyer v Buckhurst Park*

Properties (Mangal) Ltd[1], an English case followed in Australia, the court established the requirements for apparent authority:

- the representation must be made by a person with actual authority to make it,
- the third party must rely on that representation, and
- the third party must have altered their position.

4.2.3 Issue by Freight Forwarders and NVOCCs

Freight forwarders occupy a unique position, sometimes acting as agents for shippers and sometimes as principals offering carriage services. When a forwarder acts as carrier (issuing "house bills" as discussed in Chapter 3), they issue bills in their own right and are bound as carriers. When acting merely as agents, they issue bills on behalf of the actual ocean carrier.

NVOCCs (Non-Vessel Operating Common Carriers) are entities that offer carriage services without operating vessels. They issue bills of lading to shippers and consolidate cargo for carriage by actual ocean carriers. The NVOCC's bill may be a "house bill" while the ocean carrier issues a "master bill" to the NVOCC. The NVOCC is the carrier for purposes of its bill to the shipper, even though it sub-contracts the actual ocean carriage.

The distinction matters for cargo claims. A cargo owner holding an NVOCC's bill has a contract with the NVOCC, not directly with the ocean carrier. If goods are damaged, the cargo owner must look to the NVOCC, though the NVOCC may in turn have a claim against the ocean carrier under the master bill.

4.2.4 Signature Requirements

For a bill of lading to be valid, it must be signed by or on behalf of the carrier.

Article III rule 3 of the Hague-Visby Rules, as implemented in Schedule 1A to the Carriage of Goods by Sea Act 1991 (Cth), provides that after receiving goods, the carrier or master shall, on demand of the shipper, issue a bill of lading which shall be signed by the master or a named agent for the carrier.

---

[1] [1964] 2 QB 480

The requirement for signature serves several purposes. It provides evidence that the carrier or an authorised representative has verified and approved the contents of the bill. It creates a formal acknowledgment of the carrier's obligation. It helps prevent fraud by requiring a responsible person to authenticate the document.

Modern practice accepts various forms of signature. An original handwritten signature is traditional but not always necessary. Printed signatures may be valid if authorised and accepted in the trade. Electronic signatures are increasingly used, particularly with electronic bills of lading, and are recognised under the Electronic Transactions Act 1999 (Cth) subject to certain requirements.

The signature must identify who has signed on behalf of the carrier. Bills typically include a signature line stating "signed for and on behalf of [carrier name]" followed by the signature and often a stamp or notation identifying the agent's name and authority. If the signatory's authority is unclear, disputes may arise about whether the carrier is bound.

4.2.5 Pre-Printed and Stamped Bills

Many liner operators use pre-printed bill of lading forms containing standard terms. These forms include the carrier's name and logo, with spaces for cargo details, vessel information, and signatures. The use of a carrier's pre-printed form is evidence that the document is issued with the carrier's authority, though it is not conclusive, and the carrier might argue the form was improperly used.

Stamped signatures and company stamps are common on bills of lading. A rubber stamp signature may be valid if used with the carrier's authority, though it presents greater risk of forgery than original signatures. Many carriers use combinations of stamps and handwritten signatures for security. The key question is always whether the person affixing the stamp or signature had authority to bind the carrier.

4.2.6 Liability for Wrongful Issue

A person who wrongfully issues a bill of lading without authority may incur liability. If someone purporting to act for a carrier issues a bill when no goods were actually shipped (a "fictitious" bill), or when goods were shipped but the person lacked authority to issue the bill, various parties may be harmed.

A shipper who pays freight based on a fictitious bill, or a buyer who pays for goods based on a bill that proves false, may have claims for fraud or misrepresentation against the issuer. The purported carrier whose name appears on an unauthorised bill may disclaim liability, but may face reputational harm and may be estopped from denying liability if it has held out the unauthorised person as having authority.

Under Australian law, fraudulent issuance of bills of lading may constitute criminal offenses. The use of a false document to obtain property or financial advantage may be prosecuted under Commonwealth or State criminal legislation. Civil liability may also arise in tort for fraud, negligent misstatement, or under the Australian Consumer Law for misleading and deceptive conduct.

4.3 Date and Place of Issue

4.3.1 The Importance of Dating

The date stated on a bill of lading is critical for several reasons. It determines when the contract of carriage was concluded, when risk may have passed under the sale contract, whether shipment obligations have been met, and when time begins to run for various purposes including limitation periods for claims.

In documentary credit transactions, the shipment date stated in the bill must fall within the shipment period specified in the credit. If the bill is dated later than permitted, the bank will reject it as non-complying. Buyers and sellers therefore have keen interest in the date appearing on bills.

Under Article III rule 3 of the Hague-Visby Rules, when goods are loaded on board, the carrier must issue a "shipped" bill of lading showing the date when goods were actually shipped. For received for shipment bills, when an on-board notation is added, that notation must show the date of loading. The carrier has a legal obligation to state the true date. Backdating or forward-dating bills to accommodate shippers violates this obligation.

4.3.2 Dating Fraud and Backdating

Despite the legal prohibition, backdating of bills (issuing bills with earlier dates than when goods were actually loaded) occurs in practice, usually at the shipper's request to meet documentary credit deadlines. This practice, like issuing clean bills for damaged cargo, is fraudulent and exposes carriers to significant risks.

If a carrier issues a backdated bill, the carrier makes a false statement that may induce reliance by innocent third parties. A buyer who purchases goods based on a bill showing timely shipment may suffer loss if the late shipment causes problems (such as goods missing a market window or violating import restrictions). The carrier may be liable for losses flowing from the false dating.

Australian courts, following English authorities such as **Standard Chartered Bank v Pakistan National Shipping Corp*[2], have confirmed that carriers who knowingly issue backdated bills may be liable in the tort of deceit to parties who suffer loss by relying on the false date. This includes banks that pay against backdated bills in documentary credit transactions.

The fact that the carrier issued the backdated bill at the shipper's request and may hold a letter of indemnity from the shipper does not protect the carrier from third-party claims. As discussed in Chapter 3, letters of indemnity for issuing false bills are unenforceable as contrary to public policy.

The carrier cannot recover under an LOI for losses incurred through its own fraudulent conduct.

4.3.3 Place of Issue

Bills of lading typically state the place where they were issued, which is usually the port of loading.

The place of issue may be relevant for determining questions of jurisdiction and applicable law. Many bills include jurisdiction clauses specifying which courts have jurisdiction over disputes, but in the absence of such clauses, the place of issue may influence where proceedings can be brought.

---

[2] [2002] UKHL 43

Under the Carriage of Goods by Sea Act 1991 (Cth), Australian courts have jurisdiction over claims relating to carriage to or from Australian ports. Section 9 of the Act provides that the Hague-Visby Rules apply to carriage from any Australian port to a port in another country, and to carriage from a port in another country to an Australian port. The place of issue affects which national courts, and which legal regime apply to the contract.

4.4 Number of Originals

4.4.1 The Traditional Set of Three

Historically, bills of lading were issued in sets of multiple originals, typically three.

Each original is a valid bill, with any one sufficient to claim delivery of the goods. The practice of multiple originals developed because of the risk of documents being lost in transit, particularly when sent by sea mail or carried on vessels that might sink.

A typical bill of lading contains language such as "one of which being accomplished, the others to stand void." This means that once goods are delivered against presentation of one original, the other originals become worthless. The carrier is protected from delivering goods multiple times by this provision. Delivery against one original discharges the carrier's obligation.

Article III rule 4 of the Hague-Visby Rules addresses multiple originals, providing that every bill of lading shall be issued in a set where customary or requested by the shipper. Each original in the set must be numbered, and the number of originals must be stated in each document. This requirement helps prevent fraud and ensures parties know how many originals exist.

4.4.2 Risks of Multiple Originals

While multiple originals provide security against loss, they also create risks. If different originals come into different hands, disputes may arise about who is entitled to delivery. In fraud scenarios, a dishonest party might transfer different originals to different buyers, each believing they have acquired valid title to the goods.

To reduce these risks, it is common practice for all originals to be sent together in one envelope or package. Alternatively, one original might be sent directly while the others follow by separate means. Banks in documentary credit transactions typically require presentation of a "full set" of originals, ensuring that all originals are accounted for.

Problems arise when different originals are transferred to different parties through separate endorsements. Australian courts follow the principle that the first person to take in good faith and for value has priority, but determining who took first can be difficult. The carrier who delivers against one original is generally protected if it acts in good faith, but may face competing claims from holders of other originals.

4.4.3 Modern Practice and Single Bills

Modern shipping practice increasingly favours issuing bills in sets of one original rather than three. With reliable electronic communications, courier services, and the possibility of electronic bills, the historical justification for multiple originals has diminished. The risks of multiple originals in fraudulent scenarios have led many carriers to issue single originals unless specifically requested otherwise.

Documentary credit practice under UCP 600 accommodates bills issued as a single original. Article 20 provides that a bill of lading may be issued in any number of originals, and if issued in more than one original, the full set must be presented. This flexibility allows commerce to operate efficiently whether bills are issued in sets or as singles.

Electronic bills of lading eliminate the issue of multiple originals entirely. An electronic bill exists as a unique digital record that cannot be duplicated in the same way paper originals can. Transfer of the electronic bill transfers the unique record, avoiding the risks associated with multiple paper originals.

4.4.4 Copies versus Originals

It is essential to distinguish between originals and copies of bills of lading. Originals are the documents against which delivery may be claimed, while copies are for information purposes only and do not confer rights to delivery. Originals are typically marked "ORIGINAL" and signed, while copies are marked "COPY" or "NON-NEGOTIABLE COPY."

Carriers often issue numerous copies of bills for various purposes. The shipper may need copies for customs, for internal records, or for providing information to buyers. However, only originals function as documents of title. A person holding only copies cannot demand delivery from the carrier, and transfer of copies does not transfer ownership or rights in the goods.

Confusion between originals and copies can lead to problems. If a carrier mistakenly delivers goods against a copy rather than requiring presentation of an original, the carrier may be liable for misdelivery. The lawful holder of the original can sue the carrier for delivering without proper authority, even if the person who received delivery was in fact the rightful owner.

4.5 Transfer and Negotiation of Bills of Lading

4.5.1 Transferability as a Defining Feature

The ability to transfer bills of lading, passing rights to the goods and rights under the contract of carriage, is central to their commercial utility. This transferability distinguishes negotiable bills from non-negotiable transport documents and enables the document of title function discussed in Chapter 2.

Not all bills are transferable. As examined in Chapter 3, order bills (those made out "to order" or "to the order of [named party]") are transferable by endorsement and delivery.

Straight bills (consigned directly to a named consignee) are generally not transferable. The named consignee has rights but cannot transfer them by transferring the bill. Bearer bills are transferable by delivery alone without endorsement.

The law governing transfer of bills of lading in Australia derives from both common law and statute.

At common law, the transfer of a bill of lading passes constructive possession of the goods and may pass property in the goods depending on the intention of the parties. Statutorily, section 11 of the *Carriage of Goods by Sea Act 1991 (Cth)* provides for transfer of rights of suit under the contract of carriage to the lawful holder of the bill.

4.5.2 Methods of Transfer

The method of transferring a bill depends on its type. For an order bill, transfer requires both endorsement and delivery. The endorsement is a signature on the back of the bill by the current holder, which may be accompanied by words of transfer such as "deliver to [name]" or may be a blank endorsement consisting of just the signature.

A blank endorsement (signature without naming a transferee) makes the bill transferable by delivery alone from that point forward, and it effectively converts an order bill into something similar to a bearer bill. Any person who receives the bill following a blank endorsement can take by delivery without requiring further endorsement, though they may add a restrictive endorsement if desired.

A special endorsement names the transferee, such as "deliver to ABC Company." The bill remains an order bill, and ABC Company must endorse it again to transfer to another party. Special endorsements maintain tighter control over the chain of transfer but require additional formalities for each transfer.

Delivery of the bill means physical transfer of possession. The transferor must give up possession, and the transferee must take possession. Delivery may occur directly (hand to hand) or constructively (such as when a bill is deposited with a bank as agent for the buyer). Delivery without endorsement (where endorsement is required) does not effectively transfer the bill - both elements are necessary.

4.5.3 The Concept of "Lawful Holder"

Section 11 of the *Carriage of Goods by Sea Act 1991 (Cth)* uses the term "lawful holder" to identify who has rights under a bill of lading. Subsection 11(2) defines lawful holder as a person in possession of the bill who, in good faith, has become the holder either:

(a) by virtue of being the person identified in the bill as the person to whom delivery of the goods is to be made; or

(b) by virtue of one or more transfers of the bill that was effected (whether before or after the person became holder) when the bill was a sea carriage document.

This definition encompasses both the original named consignee and subsequent transferees who take through proper transfer. The requirement of good faith ensures that persons who take with knowledge of defects in title or through fraudulent means do not qualify as lawful holders entitled to statutory rights.

The definition of lawful holder determines who can enforce the contract of carriage against the carrier. Only a lawful holder has the statutory right to sue, though other parties may have rights at common law. Understanding who qualifies as a lawful holder is essential for determining who can bring cargo claims.

4.5.4 Effect of Transfer on Rights

When a bill of lading is properly transferred to a lawful holder, several legal consequences follow.

First, the holder acquires the right to possession of the goods. They can demand delivery from the carrier upon arrival at destination. This right derives from the common law recognition of the bill as a document of title.

Second, under section 11 of the *Carriage of Goods by Sea Act 1991 (Cth)*, rights of suit under the contract of carriage are transferred to the lawful holder. Subsection 11(1) provides: "Where a person becomes the lawful holder of a bill of lading, there are transferred to and vested in the person by virtue of becoming the holder all rights of suit under the contract of carriage as if the person had been a party to that contract."

This statutory transfer of rights of suit solved the historical common law problem where transferees of bills obtained possession rights but not contractual rights to sue carriers. The legislation creates a direct contractual relationship between the lawful holder and the carrier, regardless of whether the holder was the original shipper.

Third, the transfer may pass property (ownership) in the goods, though this is not automatic.

Whether property passes depends on the intention of the parties to the sale as determined by the Sale of Goods legislation and the terms of their contract. In many international sales, particularly CIF contracts, property passes when the seller transfers the bill of lading to the buyer, but this is a rule of presumed intention that may be displaced by contrary evidence.

4.5.5 Transfer of Liabilities

While rights transfer with the bill of lading, the position regarding liabilities is more complex. At common law, liabilities under contracts do not automatically transfer with assignment of rights. However, section 11(3) of the *Carriage of Goods by Sea Act 1991 (Cth)* addresses this by providing that when a person becomes a lawful holder and takes or demands delivery, they become subject to the same liabilities under the contract as if they had been a party to it.

This means the transferee becomes liable for freight and other charges due under the contract. The trigger is taking or demanding delivery. A mere receipt of the bill does not impose liability, but acting on it by claiming the goods does. This protects parties who may receive bills in intermediate positions (such as banks holding bills as security) from becoming liable for freight before they decide to take delivery.

The subsection also provides that becoming holder does not extinguish any rights or liabilities of the original shipper. The shipper remains potentially liable for freight and other obligations unless the carrier has agreed to release them. In practice, carriers often require payment of freight before releasing goods, ensuring recovery regardless of who eventually claims delivery.

4.5.6 Invalidity of Transfer

A transfer may be invalid or ineffective in various circumstances. If the transferor did not have good title to the bill (for example, if they acquired it through theft or fraud), they cannot pass good title to a subsequent transferee. However, the law protects bona fide purchasers for value without notice. A good faith transferee who gives value may acquire better title than the transferor had.

This protection derives from the negotiable character of bills of lading. Unlike ordinary contracts where assignees take "subject to equities" (affected by all defences available against the assignor), negotiable instruments can pass free from defects in earlier holders' titles if taken in good faith and for value. Bills of lading, though not negotiable instruments in the strict commercial law sense, partake of similar characteristics in protecting good faith transferees.

Transfer may also be ineffective if formalities are not observed. An order bill transferred without endorsement does not pass good title, as the transferee is not the lawful holder. Similarly, a forged endorsement does not constitute valid transfer, and the bill remains the property of the person whose signature was forged, and subsequent transfers based on the forged endorsement are invalid.

4.5.7 Transfer in Documentary Credit Transactions

Bills of lading play a crucial role in documentary credit (letter of credit) transactions, and their transfer in this context deserves special attention. In a typical documentary credit, the seller ships goods and obtains a bill of lading, then presents the bill along with other documents to a bank to obtain payment. The bank then forwards the documents to the buyer or the buyer's bank.

The presentation and transfer of bills in documentary credits is governed by UCP 600[3], which sets standards for examining documents. Banks must verify that bills conform to the credit requirements regarding description of goods, shipment dates, parties named, and other terms. If bills are conforming, banks must honour the credit by paying the seller.

When the bank pays against documents, the bill of lading is typically endorsed to the bank or to the bank's order, giving the bank control of the goods as security. Once the buyer pays or arranges payment, the bank releases the bill to the buyer, who can then claim delivery. This documentary exchange ensures that the seller receives payment while the buyer obtains control of the goods through the bill of lading.

Problems arise when bills are transferred outside the documentary credit procedure or when discrepancies exist. If a seller transfers a bill directly to a

---

[3] Uniform Customs and Practice for Documentary Credits

buyer before presenting to the bank, the bank loses its security. If the bill has discrepancies, the bank may reject it, leaving the seller with goods shipped but unpaid for. Strict compliance with documentary credit procedures is essential to maintain the security the system provides.

4.5.8 Electronic Transfer

With electronic bills of lading, transfer occurs through electronic means rather than physical delivery. Different electronic systems use different mechanisms. In registry-based systems like Bolero, transfer is effected by notifying the central registry, which updates its records to show the new holder. In blockchain-based systems, transfer occurs through a blockchain transaction that changes ownership of the digital token representing the bill.

The legal effect of electronic transfer should replicate physical transfer, in that the new holder should acquire the same rights as if they had received a paper bill through endorsement and delivery. Electronic systems achieve this through contractual arrangements among participants agreeing to treat electronic transfers as equivalent to paper transfers.

Section 11 of the *Carriage of Goods by Sea Act 1991 (Cth)* does not expressly address electronic bills, but its references to a person becoming "the holder" of a bill could potentially accommodate electronic equivalents. The *Electronic Transactions Act 1999 (Cth)* provides general support for electronic transactions, though gaps remain in expressly recognising electronic bills as documents of title.

As electronic bills become more prevalent, legislative clarification may be needed to ensure that electronic transfers have the same legal effect as paper transfers. The Rotterdam Rules provide such a framework in their provisions on electronic transport records, which could serve as a model for Australian reform if adopted.

4.6 Delivery Against Bills of Lading

4.6.1 The Carrier's Obligation

The carrier's fundamental obligation under a bill of lading is to deliver the goods to the person entitled to receive them upon presentation of the bill. This obligation is central to the document of title function - the carrier must not deliver except against surrender of an original bill of lading properly endorsed if necessary.

Article III rule 4 of the *Hague-Visby Rules* does not expressly state the delivery obligation, but it is implicit in the definition of a bill of lading. Section 11 of the *Carriage of Goods by Sea Act 1991 (Cth)* defines a bill as a document "by which the carrier undertakes to deliver the goods against surrender of the document." This makes clear that delivery is conditional on presentation of the bill.

The requirement for presentation protects all parties. It ensures that the person claiming goods is the lawful holder of the bill. It prevents multiple deliveries against different originals. It maintains the integrity of the documentary chain that supports trade finance. Carriers who deliver without requiring presentation risk liability for misdelivery.

4.6.2 Who is Entitled to Delivery

The person entitled to delivery is the lawful holder of the bill of lading. For an order bill, this is the person to whom the bill has been properly endorsed and delivered, or the person named in the last endorsement if a special endorsement was used. For a straight bill, it is the named consignee. For a bearer bill, it is the bearer in possession.

The carrier must verify that the person presenting the bill is the person entitled. For order bills, this requires checking the chain of endorsements to ensure it is complete and that the presenter is the last endorsee or the holder following a blank endorsement. The carrier must also verify the presenter's identity to ensure they are the person named in an endorsement.

This verification obligation has limits. The carrier is not required to investigate whether endorsements are genuine or whether transferees gave value or took in good faith. These are matters between transferors and transferees. The carrier's duty is to verify that the documentary chain appears regular and that the presenter has apparent authority to receive delivery.

4.6.3 Consequences of Misdelivery

Delivering goods without requiring presentation of the bill, or delivering to someone other than the lawful holder, constitutes misdelivery for which the carrier is strictly liable. The carrier cannot defend by showing that delivery was made to the actual owner of the goods if that owner was not the lawful holder of the bill. The right to delivery flows from the bill, not from ownership.

In *Sze Hai Tong Bank Ltd v Rambler Cycle Co Ltd*[4], a Privy Council decision that has been followed in Australia, the carrier delivered goods without requiring presentation of the bill, arguing that delivery was made to the actual owner and buyer of the goods. The court held this was no defence. Delivery without the bill was a fundamental breach entitling the lawful holder to damages.

The measure of damages for misdelivery is typically the full value of the goods. The carrier cannot rely on limitation of liability provisions in the *Hague-Visby Rules* or in the bill of lading terms because misdelivery is a breach going to the root of the contract. In *Motis Exports Ltd v Dampskibsselskabet AF 1912* [5], followed in Australia, the court confirmed that deliberate delivery without production of bills deprives carriers of the right to limit liability.

Carriers therefore face severe consequences for misdelivery. Even if goods are delivered to the person who in fact owns them, if that delivery is made without presentation of the bill, the carrier is liable to the lawful holder. This strict rule maintains the integrity of bills of lading as documents of title and protects the documentary system supporting international trade.

4.6.4 Delivery Without Bills: Commercial Pressure and Letters of Indemnity

Despite the legal rule requiring presentation of bills, commercial pressure often forces carriers to deliver without bills. In containerised shipping, vessels frequently arrive at destination ports before bills of lading reach the consignee, particularly when documents are sent by mail or courier. Goods may sit at expensive terminals incurring demurrage charges while waiting for documents.

To resolve this, carriers developed the practice of delivering against letters of indemnity (LOIs) issued by the consignee, often counter-guaranteed by a reputable bank. The LOI undertakes to indemnify the carrier against any claims arising from delivering without the bill. In exchange, the carrier releases cargo without requiring presentation.

---

[4] [1959] AC 576

[5] 1912* [2000] 1 Lloyd's Rep 211

This practice, while commercially understandable, is legally problematic. Delivering without bills breaches the contract of carriage and exposes the carrier to liability to the lawful holder. If the person receiving delivery is not in fact entitled (for example, because the bill has been sold to another party), the carrier faces claims for misdelivery and the LOI may provide inadequate protection.

Courts have held that letters of indemnity do not prevent carriers from being liable for misdelivery; they merely provide a contractual right to claim reimbursement from the indemnifier. In *Motis Exports v Dampskibsselskabet*[6], the court emphasised that an LOI does not convert wrongful delivery into rightful delivery. The carrier remains liable to the lawful bill holder, though it may recover from the indemnifier.

Furthermore, LOIs may be unenforceable if delivery without bills involves fraud or if the indemnifier knows the goods belong to someone other than the receiver. Courts refuse to enforce indemnities supporting fraudulent conduct. The carrier may therefore be left exposed, unable to recover under the LOI while liable for the full value of goods to the lawful holder.

The problems with delivering against LOIs have led to calls for reform and to increased use of electronic bills of lading, which can be transmitted almost instantaneously and eliminate the problem of documents arriving after vessels. However, delivering against LOIs remains common practice despite the legal risks, reflecting the commercial realities of modern container shipping.

4.6.5 Delivery of Part of Goods

Sometimes only part of a consignment is ready for delivery, raising questions about whether the carrier can deliver part against presentation of the bill. Generally, the carrier is obliged to deliver the entire consignment evidenced by the bill. Delivering part while retaining part creates practical difficulties.

If the carrier delivers part of goods and retains the bill, the holder loses the document needed to claim the remainder. If the carrier releases the bill after partial delivery, the holder could potentially claim the remainder from a

---

[6] ibid

different person or sell the bill, defrauding the carrier. To address this, carriers may endorse the bill noting partial delivery and return it to the holder or may issue a delivery order for the remaining goods.

These practices are less than satisfactory and should be avoided where possible. The better approach is to issue separate bills for separate parcels if there is any possibility of split delivery. The complications of partial delivery illustrate the importance of matching documentary arrangements to the intended delivery pattern.

4.7 Switch Bills of Lading

Switch bills of lading are substitute bills issued to replace the original bills during the voyage. They allow the shipper or subsequent holder to substitute new bills showing different particulars, such as a different consignee, different notify party, or different description of goods, while concealing commercial information from other parties.

Switch bills are commonly used in commodity trading where goods are sold multiple times during the voyage. The seller may not want the ultimate buyer to know the origin or previous price of the goods. By obtaining switch bills that show the immediate seller as shipper rather than the original supplier, this commercial information is concealed.

The legal status of switch bills is controversial. On one view, the original bills are surrendered and cancelled when switch bills are issued, and the switch bills become the operative documents. On another view, switch bills are not "true" bills of lading because they are not issued upon receipt of goods but rather document an existing carriage for which bills were already issued.

Problems arise if both original and switch bills come into different parties' hands, each claiming to be the lawful holder. The carrier may face competing claims for delivery. Australian courts have not extensively addressed switch bills, but English authorities suggest that the first person to present a valid bill in good faith is entitled to delivery, and the carrier who delivers to that person is protected.

Carriers exercise caution with switch bills given these uncertainties. Many carriers require surrender of all originals of the first set before issuing switch bills. Carriers also limit the number of switches permitted and may refuse to issue switch bills in certain circumstances. Despite the commercial demand for switch bills in commodity trading, their use presents legal risks for all parties.

4.8 Spent Bills

A bill of lading becomes "spent" when its purpose has been fulfilled, typically when goods have been delivered and the bill surrendered to the carrier. Once spent, the bill is usually stamped or marked "accomplished" to prevent reuse. The spent bill has no further function regarding those goods, though it may serve as evidence of the carriage that occurred.

Sometimes bills become spent in other ways. If goods are lost at sea, the bill no longer represents goods available for delivery, though it remains evidence of the contract and the basis for cargo claims. If goods are lawfully seized by customs or other authorities, the bill may be spent as a document of title though the carrier's obligations continue.

The concept of spent bills is important in multi-stop voyages where goods are discharged at intermediate ports. Once discharge occurs, the bill relating to those goods is spent for that portion. If the same bill covers goods for multiple destinations (which is unusual), it becomes progressively spent as parcels are discharged.

4.9 Conclusion

The issue and transfer of bills of lading are governed by a complex body of rules derived from statute, common law, and commercial practice. Proper issuance requires authority, accurate dating, correct signature, and compliance with formal requirements. Transfer requires observance of endorsement and delivery formalities for order bills, with legal consequences flowing from the transfer including passing of possession rights, property (depending on intention), and rights of suit under statute.

Understanding these principles is essential for all participants in maritime commerce. Carriers must ensure bills are properly issued and delivered only against proper presentation. Shippers must verify that bills accurately reflect their shipments and are issued by authorised agents. Banks must examine bills for compliance with documentary credit requirements. Buyers must ensure bills are properly transferred to them and that they can enforce their rights against carriers.

The next chapters will examine what bills state about goods (Chapter 5), how bills function as evidence of the contract of carriage (Chapter 6), and the specific obligations and rights regarding delivery (Chapter 8). The procedural aspects covered in this chapter provide the foundation for understanding the substantive rights and obligations that bills of lading create and evidence.

Chapter 5: The Bill of Lading as a Receipt

5.1 Introduction

Among the three primary functions of the bill of lading, its role as a receipt for goods is the most straightforward yet also gives rise to some of the most contentious disputes in shipping law.

The statements made in a bill of lading about the quantity, description, and condition of goods have significant commercial and legal consequences. They influence sales transactions, documentary credit operations, insurance coverage, and carrier liability. This chapter examines the bill of lading's receipt function under Australian law, including the legal effect of statements in bills, the carrier's duties and limitations regarding those statements, and the practice of clausing bills.

The receipt function is governed by both contractual principles and statutory provisions in the Hague-Visby Rules as implemented by the Carriage of Goods by Sea Act 1991 (Cth). Article III rule 3 of the Hague-Visby Rules sets out detailed requirements for what bills of lading must state, while rule 4 addresses the evidential effect of those statements. Understanding these provisions and their interpretation by Australian courts is essential for all parties dealing with bills of lading.

5.2 Statutory Requirements for Bill of Lading Statements

5.2.1 Article III Rule 3 Requirements

Article III rule 3 of the *Hague-Visby Rules*, contained in Schedule 1A to the *Carriage of Goods by Sea Act 1991 (Cth)*, establishes the carrier's obligation regarding statements in bills of lading. After receiving goods into his charge, the carrier, master, or agent of the carrier shall, on demand of the shipper, issue a bill of lading showing:

(a) The leading marks necessary for identification of the goods as furnished in writing by the shipper before the loading begins, provided such marks are stamped or otherwise shown clearly upon the goods if uncovered, or on the cases or coverings in which such goods are contained, in such a manner as should ordinarily remain legible until the end of the voyage;

(b) Either the number of packages or pieces, or the quantity, or weight, as the case may be, as furnished in writing by the shipper;

(c) The apparent order and condition of the goods.

These requirements create a framework for what bills must state. However, as we shall see, the carrier's duty to make these statements is subject to important qualifications and limitations.

5.2.2 Leading Marks

Leading marks are identifying marks or numbers that distinguish particular goods or packages. In traditional break-bulk cargo operations, each package might be stencilled or labelled with marks such as "ABC Company, Package 1 of 50, Hamburg." These marks allow identification among multiple shippers' goods carried on the same vessel.

The carrier's duty regarding marks is limited. The carrier must show marks furnished by the shipper in writing, and only if those marks are clearly displayed on the goods themselves or their containers in a manner likely to remain legible. The carrier is not obliged to create or verify marks; the obligation is to record what the shipper has provided and what is visible.

In modern containerised shipping, marks have less significance because goods are sealed in containers. The container number becomes the primary identifier. Bills of lading for containerised cargo typically state the container number and may include "shipper's load and count" notations indicating that the carrier has no knowledge of marks on goods within the sealed container.

5.2.3 Quantity: Number, Weight, or Volume

The bill must state the quantity of goods, expressed as number of packages or pieces, or as weight or volume. This is critical information for buyers, insurers, and carriers. It determines the value at stake, influences limitation calculations under Article IV rule 5, and provides the basis for detecting shortages upon delivery.

The carrier's obligation regarding quantity is "as furnished in writing by the shipper." This means the carrier records what the shipper declares. For goods the carrier can count or weigh, the carrier should verify the shipper's figures.

For sealed containers, the carrier has limited ability to verify and typically qualifies statements with "shipper's load and count."

Article III rule 3 contains an important proviso: the carrier is not bound to state marks, number, quantity, or weight which it has reasonable grounds for suspecting do not accurately represent the goods actually received, or which it has no reasonable means of checking. This proviso is examined in detail below.

5.2.4 Apparent Order and Condition

The requirement to state "apparent order and condition" of goods is unique because it derives from the carrier's own observation rather than shipper-supplied information. The carrier must note any visible defects, damage, or irregularities in the goods or packaging as received.

The word "apparent" is significant. The carrier is obliged to note only what is visible or should be detected by reasonable inspection. The carrier need not open sealed packages or use special equipment to detect hidden defects. For containerised cargo delivered as sealed units, the carrier can observe only the external condition of the container, not the contents within.

If goods appear to be in good order and condition when received, the bill is issued "clean" without clausing. If defects are apparent, the carrier should note them, creating a "claused" or "unclean" bill as discussed in Chapter 3. The apparent order and condition statement is entirely the carrier's responsibility, and shippers cannot dictate what the carrier observes.

Australian courts have emphasised that carriers must exercise reasonable care in observing condition. In *The "David Agmashenebeli"* [2003] 1 Lloyd's Rep 92, a case involving similar provisions, the court held that carriers must make reasonable inspection but are not required to conduct detailed examinations. This principle has been applied in Australian jurisprudence to define the scope of the carrier's inspection duty.

5.3 Qualifications and Limitations on Carrier's Statements

5.3.1 The Article III Rule 3 Proviso

Article III rule 3 contains a critical proviso allowing carriers to qualify their statements: "Provided that no carrier, master or agent of the carrier shall be bound to state or show in the bill of lading any marks, number, quantity, or weight which he has reasonable ground for suspecting not accurately to represent the goods actually received, or which he has had no reasonable means of checking."

This proviso recognises that carriers cannot always verify shipper-supplied information. It permits carriers to qualify statements or omit them entirely if verification is impossible or if the carrier suspects inaccuracy. The proviso applies only to marks, number, quantity, and weight not to apparent order and condition, which the carrier must always observe.

The proviso protects carriers in two situations. First, where the carrier has reasonable grounds for suspecting that shipper-supplied information is inaccurate. For example, if packages appear to be fewer than declared, or lighter than stated weights would suggest, the carrier may qualify the statement or refuse to include it.

Second, where the carrier has no reasonable means of checking the information. This is particularly relevant for containerised cargo. If goods are packed and sealed by the shipper in a container, the carrier has no reasonable means of verifying the contents. The carrier may therefore qualify statements about quantity or description of contents.

The burden is on the carrier to establish that it had reasonable grounds for suspicion or no reasonable means of checking. Carriers cannot routinely qualify all statements as a matter of policy. Each case depends on its particular circumstances. If the carrier qualifies statements without justification, the qualification may be ineffective.

5.3.2 "Shipper's Load and Count" and Similar Clauses

The most common qualification in modern bills of lading is "shipper's load and count" or variations such as "said to contain," "shipper's weight," or "contents unknown." These clauses indicate that information about quantity or description comes from the shipper, not from the carrier's own knowledge or verification.

Such clauses are permissible under the Article III rule 3 proviso where the carrier has no reasonable means of checking. For sealed containers packed by shippers, Australian courts have recognised that carriers cannot verify contents and may use these qualifications. In *Ace Imports Pty Ltd v Companhia de Navegao Lloyd Brasileiro* [7], the New South Wales Court of Appeal held that "shipper's load and count" clauses are effective to limit the carrier's acknowledgment regarding quantity when used in circumstances where the carrier genuinely cannot verify.

However, the effectiveness of such clauses has limits. If the carrier does have means of checking (for example, if containers are loaded in the carrier's presence or if weight can be verified by weighing the container), the qualification may not protect the carrier. The clause must reflect genuine inability to verify, not mere convenience.

Furthermore, qualification clauses do not relieve carriers from all responsibility. Even with a "said to contain" clause, if shortages are obvious (for example, if a container appears damaged or is visibly lighter than it should be), the carrier may be expected to investigate. The carrier cannot use qualification clauses to avoid responsibilities that reasonable inspection would reveal.

5.3.3 Extent of Carrier's Inspection Duty

The extent of the carrier's duty to inspect goods and verify statements is a question of reasonableness. The carrier must exercise the care that a prudent carrier would exercise in the circumstances. This varies depending on the type of cargo, the shipping practice in the relevant trade, and what is visible or ascertainable.

For break-bulk cargo loaded in the carrier's presence, greater inspection is expected. The carrier should count packages, observe their apparent condition, and verify marks. If goods are delivered to the carrier already packaged and sealed, less intensive inspection is required; the carrier need only examine the external condition and cannot be expected to open packages.

---

[7] (1987) 10 NSWLR 32

For containerised cargo, the inspection duty is minimal where containers are received already sealed. The carrier can inspect the external condition of the container, verify the container number, and perhaps weigh the loaded container, but cannot reasonably be expected to verify contents. This limitation is recognised in the case law and reflects practical shipping realities.

Australian courts apply an objective standard of reasonableness. In El Greco (Australia) Pty Ltd v Mediterranean Shipping Co SA [8], the Federal Court considered what inspection was reasonable for containerised cargo. The court recognised that carriers receiving sealed containers could not verify contents and could appropriately use qualification clauses but emphasised that carriers must still exercise reasonable care regarding matters they can observe.

5.3.4 Limitations Regarding Specialised or Technical Goods

Special difficulties arise with goods requiring technical knowledge or specialised inspection. For example, machinery, electronic equipment, or chemicals may appear in good condition externally while having defects detectable only by expert examination. Carriers are not expected to employ experts to inspect all cargo.

The "apparent" order and condition requirement addresses this. Carriers need only note defects that are visible to a reasonably careful observer. If technical defects exist but are not apparent, the carrier is not responsible for noting them. The shipper bears the risk that hidden defects may exist despite the clean bill.

This principle extends to goods in specialised packaging. If goods are in sealed drums, wrapped pallets, or factory-sealed cartons, the carrier cannot see the actual goods. A clean bill in such cases means the packaging appeared to be in good order and condition, not that the goods within were necessarily satisfactory.

5.4 Evidential Effect of Bill of Lading Statements

---

[8] [2004] FCA 202

5.4.1 Article III Rule 4: Prima Facie Evidence

Article III rule 4 of the Hague-Visby Rules addresses the evidential effect of statements in bills of lading. It provides: "Such a bill of lading shall be prima facie evidence of the receipt by the carrier of the goods as therein described in accordance with paragraphs 3(a), (b) and (c)."

This means the bill is prima facie (first sight) evidence of what it states regarding marks, quantity, and apparent order and condition. The carrier has acknowledged receiving goods as described, and in litigation, the bill creates a presumption to that effect. The burden falls on the carrier to prove that goods were not as described if the carrier wishes to deny the statements.

However, the provision states only "prima facie" evidence, not conclusive evidence. The carrier can rebut the presumption by producing contrary evidence. If the carrier can prove that goods were not received as stated in the bill, the carrier may escape liability based on those statements.

The prima facie evidential effect applies in disputes between the original contracting parties (shipper and carrier). As between these parties, the bill is merely evidence that may be contradicted. The shipper might prove that goods actually delivered differed from what the bill stated, or the carrier might prove that goods received differed from what the shipper claimed.

5.4.2 Article III Rule 4: Conclusive Evidence as Against Third Parties

The second part of Article III rule 4 provides much stronger protection for third parties: "However, proof to the contrary shall not be admissible when the bill of lading has been transferred to a third party acting in good faith."

This creates conclusive evidence - evidence that cannot be contradicted when the bill has been transferred to a good faith third party. The carrier cannot prove against such a third party that goods were different from what the bill states. The third party is entitled to rely absolutely on the statements in the bill.

This protection is essential to the negotiability and document of title function of bills of lading. Third parties who purchase goods or advance money based on bills of lading must be able to rely on the statements without investigating what might have actually been shipped. If carriers could contradict their own statements in bills, the security and certainty needed for international trade would be undermined.

The phrase "third party acting in good faith" requires the transferee to take without knowledge of any inaccuracy in the bill. A transferee who knows that goods were not as described cannot invoke the conclusive evidence rule. However, the burden is on the carrier to prove the transferee's bad faith, which is difficult. Mere suspicion or opportunity to discover inaccuracies does not constitute bad faith.

Australian courts have applied this principle rigorously. In Grant v Norway [9], an early English case that has been followed in Australia, the House of Lords held that a shipowner who authorised the master to sign bills of lading was bound by those bills even when they falsely stated that goods had been shipped. The owner could not deny the truth of the bill against an innocent purchaser who relied on it.

5.4.3 Estoppel by Representation

The conclusive evidence rule in Article III rule 4 overlaps with the common law doctrine of estoppel by representation. Where a carrier makes a statement in a bill of lading, and a third party relies on that statement to their detriment, the carrier may be estopped (prevented) from denying the truth of the statement.

The requirements for estoppel are:

(1) a clear representation of fact,
(2) intended to be acted upon or made in circumstances where it is reasonable to expect reliance,
(3) actual reliance by the representee, and
(4) detriment resulting from the reliance.

Bills of lading satisfy these requirements when transferred to third parties who give value.

Estoppel operates independently of the *Hague-Visby Rules*, though in practice the Article III rule 4 conclusive evidence provision achieves similar results. Estoppel may be broader, potentially applying even where the Rules do not

---

[9] 1851) 10 CB 665

(such as in purely domestic carriage not governed by the Act), and may create liability in tort for misrepresentation in addition to contractual liability.

Australian courts have applied estoppel principles in bill of lading cases.

In *V/O Rasnoimport v Guthrie & Co Ltd* [10], a case concerning bills that overstated quantity, the court held the carrier estopped from denying the quantity stated against an innocent purchaser of the bill. The purchaser had paid for goods based on the bill's statement and was entitled to recover the value of the shortfall.

5.4.4 Limits on Conclusive Evidence and Estoppel

While Article III rule 4 makes statements conclusive against third parties, and estoppel principles support this, there are limits. The conclusive evidence rule applies to statements about marks, quantity, and apparent order and condition as required by Article III rule 3. It does not extend to other matters that might appear in bills.

For example, statements about the nature or quality of goods beyond their apparent condition are not protected by Article III rule 4.

If a bill describes goods as "high-grade copper" but the apparent condition requirement would not extend to verifying purity, a carrier might not be estopped from proving the goods were lower grade.

Similarly, qualification clauses may limit the scope of estoppel. If a bill states "said to contain 100 cartons" with a "shipper's load and count" qualification, the carrier may not be estopped from proving a different quantity because the carrier never made an unqualified representation. The effectiveness of qualifications was discussed above.

Furthermore, estoppel requires reliance. If a third party did not in fact rely on the statement (perhaps because they independently verified the goods), estoppel may not apply. However, reliance is generally presumed where bills are transferred for value, and the carrier bears the burden of proving non-reliance.

---

[10] [1966] 1 Lloyd's Rep 1

5.4.5 Fraud and Misrepresentation

Where a carrier knowingly makes false statements in a bill of lading, the carrier may be liable in the tort of deceit (fraud) to third parties who rely on the false statements and suffer loss. This liability is separate from contractual liability and is not subject to contractual limitation clauses.

In *Standard Chartered Bank v Pakistan National Shipping Corp* [11], the House of Lords held that a carrier who knowingly issued a backdated bill of lading was liable in deceit to a bank that paid against the bill in a documentary credit transaction. The bank relied on the false shipment date to its detriment, and the carrier could not rely on limitation clauses because fraud unravels all.

Australian courts have followed this approach. Fraudulent statements in bills of lading create liability beyond the contract of carriage. Even if the carrier could limit liability for breach of contract under the *Hague-Visby Rules*, fraudulent misrepresentation creates unlimited tort liability.

The carrier's liability for fraud extends to its agents who make false statements. If a ship's master or loading agent issues a false bill with knowledge of its falsity, the carrier is vicariously liable for that fraud. The only defence is if the carrier proves the agent acted entirely outside the scope of authority, which is difficult where the agent's role involves issuing bills.

5.5 Particular Statement Categories

5.5.1 Quantity Statements and Shortages

Statements about quantity - the number of packages, weight, or volume are among the most important in bills of lading. Shortages (delivery of less than stated quantity) are among the most common cargo claims. The legal principles governing quantity statements and shortage claims are well-developed.

When a bill states a specific quantity and goods delivered are short, the prima facie evidence rule creates a presumption that the carrier received the stated quantity and is liable for the shortage. The carrier can rebut this in proceedings

---

[11] [2002] UKHL 43

with the shipper by proving that less was actually loaded. Against a third-party transferee, the carrier cannot rebut. The quantity is conclusive.

However, carriers can protect themselves through qualification clauses. A statement "said to contain 100 cartons, shipper's load and count" is not an unqualified acknowledgment of 100 cartons. If delivery reveals only 90 cartons, the carrier may defend by showing the qualification meant the carrier did not verify quantity. The effectiveness depends on whether the carrier genuinely could not verify and whether the qualification was sufficiently clear.

In Australian case law, courts have carefully examined whether qualification clauses effectively limit carriers' acknowledgments. In *Ace Imports v Lloyd Brasileiro* [12], the New South Wales Court of Appeal analysed a "shipper's load, weight and count" clause. The court held it was effective to qualify the carrier's acknowledgment where the carrier genuinely had no means of verifying the contents of sealed containers.

Weight statements create particular issues. If a bill states weight "as per shipper's declaration" or "shipper's weight," and delivered goods weigh less, the question is whether the carrier acknowledged receiving the stated weight or merely recorded the shipper's claim. Courts generally hold that qualified weight statements do not create liability for shortages unless the carrier had means of weighing and the actual weight was so different that the carrier should have noticed.

5.5.2 Description of Goods

Bills of lading describe goods in varying detail. Some provide generic descriptions like "general cargo" or "said to contain personal effects." Others provide detailed descriptions including product names, grades, specifications. The level of detail affects the carrier's liability for misdescription.

The *Hague-Visby Rules* do not expressly require bills to describe the nature of goods beyond what is necessary to identify them and state apparent condition. Detailed descriptions usually appear because shippers request them (for example, to satisfy documentary credit requirements) rather than because carriers must provide them.

---

[12] (1987) 10 NSWLR 32

When goods are delivered that do not match the description in the bill, issues arise. If the description was of apparent characteristics (such as "steel pipes" which could be verified by observation), the carrier's statement may be binding. If the description was of intrinsic qualities not apparent (such as "high-grade steel pipes"), the carrier may not have warranted those qualities.

Courts distinguish between descriptions of type and descriptions of quality. A bill stating "copper wire" describes the type of goods in a way the carrier can verify by observation. A bill stating "99.9% pure copper wire" describes quality that the carrier cannot verify without testing. The carrier is bound by type descriptions but may not be bound by quality descriptions beyond apparent condition.

Qualification clauses again play a role. If a bill states "said to contain copper wire" with appropriate qualifications, the carrier has not unequivocally described the goods as copper wire. If delivered goods prove to be a different material, the carrier may defend based on the qualification, particularly if the goods were in sealed containers.

5.5.3 Condition Statements and Damage Claims

Statements about the apparent order and condition of goods form the basis for damage claims. If a bill is issued clean (without noting defects), there is a presumption that goods were received in good order and condition. If goods are delivered damaged, the burden falls on the carrier to prove the damage occurred after loading.

The carrier's duty regarding condition is limited to apparent condition. Hidden defects, internal damage not visible externally, or deterioration that was not yet manifested when goods were loaded, are not the carrier's responsibility to note. The shipper bears the risk of latent defects that a reasonable inspection would not reveal.

For containerised cargo in sealed containers, the carrier can observe only the container's external condition. If the container appears intact when received and delivered, but goods within are damaged, the carrier may defend by showing the damage was not apparent and the container remained sealed. This defence is particularly strong where "shipper's load and count" clauses apply.

Conversely, if external damage to a container is apparent but not noted in the bill, the carrier may be liable for damage to contents even if the carrier did not see the contents. The failure to note apparent container damage may estop the carrier from denying that damage to contents occurred after loading.

Australian courts have addressed condition statements in various contexts. The principle is that carriers must note defects that reasonable inspection would reveal but are not liable for defects that were genuinely hidden and not discoverable. The test is objective - what a reasonably careful carrier would have observed.

5.5.4 Marks and Numbers

Statements about marks and numbers, while required by Article III rule 3, have less commercial significance in modern practice than in traditional break-bulk shipping. Marks identify packages among mixed cargo. In container shipping, the container number serves this function, and internal package marks are less important.

Nonetheless, mark statements create legal obligations. If a bill states specific marks and goods delivered bear different marks, questions arise about whether the correct goods were delivered. The carrier's obligation is to deliver goods matching the bill's description, including marks.

Carriers can qualify mark statements using the Article III rule 3 proviso. If marks are not clearly legible, or if the carrier cannot verify marks on goods in sealed containers, qualifications like "marks as per shipper's declaration" protect the carrier from liability for misdelivery based on mark discrepancies.

5.6 The Practice of Clausing Bills of Lading

5.6.1 When and How to Clause

As discussed in Chapter 3, bills are "claused" when the carrier notes defects, damage, or irregularities in the goods or packaging. Clausing is the carrier's mechanism for protecting against liability for pre-existing problems. It is both a legal obligation (to accurately state apparent condition) and a practical necessity (to avoid liability for damage the carrier did not cause).

Carriers should clause bills whenever:

- Packaging is visibly damaged, torn, stained, or inadequate.
- Goods (if visible) show signs of damage, deterioration, or defects.
- Quantity delivered appears to differ from shipper's declaration.
- Marks are illegible or contradictory.
- Any other irregularity is apparent.

The clause should be specific and clear. Generic clauses like "damaged" or "poor condition" are less protective than specific clauses like "three cartons crushed, contents protruding" or "drums rusted, leaking apparent." Specific clauses help prove the extent of pre-existing damage and prevent disputes about whether later-discovered damage was present at loading.

Clauses must be noted on the face of the bill or incorporated by reference in a way that makes them part of the bill's terms. Clauses noted only in the carrier's internal records or in marginal notations that are not clearly incorporated may not be effective to limit the carrier's acknowledgment in the bill itself.

5.6.2 Standard Clause Formulations

Carriers have developed standard clause formulations for common situations:

- "One package torn, contents exposed."
- "Cartons stained, possible water damage".
- "Drums rusty, condition as presented".
- "Bags torn, contents leaking".
- "Packaging inadequate for sea voyage"
- "Second-hand cases, condition uncertain"

These formulations are sufficiently specific to put cargo interests on notice while being standardised enough to apply consistently. The key is that they describe observed conditions factually and specifically.

For containerised cargo, where carriers cannot see contents, common clauses include:

- "Container received sealed, contents unknown".

- "Shipper's load, stow and count".
- "Said to contain [description], not verified."
- "Container externally damaged, contents unknown"

These clauses reflect the carrier's limited ability to inspect sealed containers while reserving rights regarding contents.

5.6.3 Disputes About Clausing

Shippers often resist clausing because claused bills are not acceptable in documentary credit transactions and may affect sale negotiations. This creates pressure on carriers to issue clean bills despite visible defects. Carriers must resist this pressure to avoid making false statements that could create liability.

If a shipper disputes proposed clausing, the carrier should:

- Document the defect with photographs or detailed written descriptions.
- Invite the shipper to inspect the goods jointly.
- Offer the shipper the opportunity to re-package or remedy the defect.
- If the shipper refuses to accept clausing, decline to issue a bill or insist on clausing despite shipper's objection.

The carrier should not issue a clean bill in exchange for a letter of indemnity where defects are genuinely apparent. As discussed in Chapter 3, such LOIs are unenforceable as contrary to public policy, and the carrier remains exposed to third-party claims based on the false clean bill.

5.6.4 Effect of Clausing on Carrier Liability

Proper clausing protects carriers from liability for pre-existing damage. If a bill notes "ten cartons water-stained," and delivered cartons show water staining, the carrier has evidence that damage pre-existed the voyage. The cargo owner cannot recover from the carrier for damage that was noted at the time of loading.

However, clausing does not provide complete protection. If damage worsens during the voyage, the carrier may be liable for the additional damage. The clause protects only against the specific defect noted. If a bill notes "one carton torn" and delivery reveals multiple cartons torn, the carrier is liable for the additional damage.

Furthermore, clausing does not excuse the carrier from proper care during carriage. If a bill notes "packaging fragile" and goods are damaged during carriage due to improper handling, the carrier is liable. The clause merely acknowledges the goods' condition at loading; it does not relieve the carrier's obligation to carry them carefully.

5.7 Special Issues in Container Shipping

5.7.1 "Shipper's Load and Count" Reconsidered

Container shipping has fundamentally altered the receipt function of bills of lading. Traditionally, carriers loaded goods and could observe quantity and condition. With containers, shippers typically pack and seal containers at inland depots. Carriers receive sealed boxes whose contents they cannot verify.

The "shipper's load and count" clause and similar qualifications are essential in this environment. They reflect commercial reality. Carriers genuinely have no means of checking container contents. Australian courts have recognised this in cases like *Ace Imports v Lloyd Brasileiro* (ibid), holding such clauses effective where carriers cannot reasonably verify contents.

However, tensions remain. Third parties acquiring bills want reliable statements about cargo. Banks want bills that confirm what is being shipped. Yet carriers cannot provide certainty about goods they have never seen. The compromise is qualification clauses that put parties on notice of the carrier's limited knowledge.

The effectiveness of "shipper's load and count" clauses continues to be tested.

Courts examine whether carriers have genuinely exercised reasonable care in the circumstances. If carriers could have checked but chose not to for convenience, qualifications may be ineffective. If carriers genuinely had no practical means of checking, qualifications are upheld.

5.7.2 Container Weight Verification

A particular issue is container weight. Overweight containers create safety risks for vessels, stevedores, and transport infrastructure. International regulations increasingly require verification of container weights (VGM - Verified Gross Mass) before loading.

Under the International Convention for the Safety of Life at Sea (SOLAS) as amended, shippers must provide verified gross mass of packed containers. This regulatory requirement operates independently of the carrier's contractual and Hague-Visby obligations regarding bill of lading statements.

The VGM requirement does not eliminate carriers' ability to qualify weight statements in bills. Even with VGM, bills often state "weight as per shipper's declaration" or similar qualifications. However, if the carrier verifies weight (whether through weighing or VGM certification), unqualified weight statements may create greater liability.

5.7.3 Container Condition Clauses

When receiving containers, carriers can and should inspect external condition. Visible damage to containers – "dents, holes, broken seals, or other defects" should be noted in the bill. This protects carriers if contents prove damaged.

Standard container condition clauses include:

- "Container delivered with broken seal".
- "Container side panel dented".
- "Container door damaged, may not be weatherproof".
- "Container floor wet, possible water ingress"

These clauses put cargo owners on notice that container integrity may be compromised, which could affect contents. They also provide evidence if disputes arise about when damage occurred.

5.8 Electronic Bills and Receipt Statements

Electronic bills of lading must replicate the receipt function of paper bills. Electronic systems must allow carriers to record statements about marks, quantity, and condition, and must ensure those statements have the same evidential effect as paper bills.

Most electronic bill systems provide electronic forms where carriers input the required information. The information becomes part of the electronic record in the same way it would appear on a paper bill. The technical challenge is ensuring the record cannot be altered after creation and is accessible to all relevant parties.

The evidential effect of statements in electronic bills depends on legal recognition of electronic documents. The Electronic Transactions Act 1999 (Cth) provides that electronic communications satisfy legal requirements for written documents if information is accessible for subsequent reference. This should support electronic bill statements having the same evidential effect as paper bills.

However, legal uncertainty remains in Australia about whether electronic bills qualify as documents of title and whether Article III rule 4's conclusive evidence provision applies to them. Legislative clarification would help, perhaps through amendments to the Carriage of Goods by Sea Act 1991 (Cth) expressly addressing electronic bills.

5.9 Interaction with Sale Contracts and Documentary Credits

5.9.1 Sale Contract Requirements

In international sales, the sale contract often specifies what the bill of lading must state. CIF (Cost, Insurance, Freight) contracts typically require bills showing the contract description of goods, shipped in good order and condition (clean bills), and dated within the shipment period.

The seller's obligation is to tender bills that comply with the contract. If the carrier issues claused bills, the seller may be unable to fulfill the contract obligations. This is why shippers pressure carriers to issue clean bills. However, the carrier's duty is to state apparent condition accurately, not to accommodate the shipper's sale contract difficulties.

If goods genuinely are not in good condition, the seller should either:

- Remedy the defects before shipment.

- Renegotiate the sale contract to accept claused bills.
- Accept that tender of claused bills may be rejected by the buyer.
- Find alternative means of documenting the sale.

The carrier should not be drawn into the shipper's commercial difficulties by issuing false clean bills. The legal risks to carriers outweigh any commercial benefit from accommodating shippers.

5.9.2 Documentary Credit Examination Standards

Under UCP 600, banks examining documents in documentary credit transactions apply strict compliance standards. Bills must conform exactly to the credit requirements. Even minor discrepancies result in rejection.

Article 27 of UCP 600 specifically provides that a transport document must not indicate that goods or packaging are defective. This means claused bills are generally not acceptable unless the credit expressly permits them. Banks have no discretion to accept claused bills if the credit requires clean bills.

Banks examine bills as documents, not as evidence of facts. A bank is not investigating whether goods were really in good condition. The bank is checking whether the bill states they were. If the bill is clean, the bank accepts it (assuming other requirements are met). If the bill is claused, the bank rejects it.

This documentary approach creates pressure throughout the chain. Buyers demand clean bills in credits to ensure they receive goods in good condition. Sellers need clean bills to get paid. Carriers face pressure to issue clean bills regardless of actual conditions. The system works only if carriers maintain integrity by accurately stating what they observe.

5.10 Conclusion

The receipt function of bills of lading, though seemingly straightforward, involves complex legal principles and practical challenges. Carriers must navigate statutory requirements in the Hague-Visby Rules, common law evidential and estoppel principles, and commercial pressures from shippers and cargo interests.

The fundamental principle is that carriers must make accurate statements about marks, quantity, and apparent condition of goods received. These statements have significant legal consequences. They create prima facie evidence against the carrier and conclusive evidence against the carrier when bills are transferred to good faith third parties.

Carriers can protect themselves through proper use of qualification clauses where they genuinely cannot verify information, and through diligent clausing when defects are apparent. However, carriers cannot avoid liability by issuing false bills, even in exchange for letters of indemnity. The legal risks of false statements, including fraud liability, loss of limitation rights, and exposure to third-party claims far exceed any commercial benefits.

For shippers and cargo interests, understanding the receipt function is essential to managing risk. Clean bills provide strong evidence of goods shipped in good condition, but only if carriers have genuinely verified condition. Qualification clauses put buyers on notice of the carrier's limited knowledge. Claused bills signal pre-existing problems that may affect value or insurability.

As we move to examine the bill of lading as evidence of the contract of carriage in Chapter 6, we will see how the receipt statements interact with contractual terms to define the parties' rights and obligations. The receipt function provides the factual foundation - what goods were shipped and in what condition, while the contract function establishes the legal framework governing their carriage.

Chapter 6: The Bill of Lading as Evidence of the Contract of Carriage

6.1 Introduction

While the bill of lading serves as a receipt for goods and a document of title, its function as evidence of the contract of carriage is equally fundamental. The bill sets out the terms and conditions governing the relationship between carrier and cargo owner, establishing rights, obligations, exceptions, and limitations that will apply throughout the carriage and beyond. This chapter examines how bills of lading evidence contracts of carriage under Australian law, the distinction between the bill and the underlying contract, and the complex issues that arise when bills incorporate terms from other documents, particularly charterparties.

Understanding the evidentiary function of bills of lading is essential because it determines what terms govern the carriage, who is bound by those terms, and how disputes about cargo loss or damage will be resolved. The position differs significantly depending on whether the bill remains with the original shipper or has been transferred to a third party, and whether the carriage involves a charterparty or operates as a standard liner shipment.

6.2 The Bill as Evidence versus The Bill as Contract

6.2.1 Formation of the Contract of Carriage

The contract of carriage is typically concluded before the bill of lading is issued. In liner shipping, the contract forms when the shipper books space on a vessel and the carrier accepts the booking. In charterparty situations, the contract is the charterparty itself. The bill of lading is subsequently issued as documentary evidence of the contract already made.

This temporal sequence is important. The bill does not create the contract; it evidences it. The actual contract may have been concluded orally, by exchange of booking confirmations, or through the charterparty. The bill records the terms of that pre-existing contract in written form.

The distinction was established in classic cases such as SS Ardennes (Cargo Owners) v SS Ardennes (Owners) [13], followed in Australia.

Lord Justice Slesser stated:

"A bill of lading is not the contract but only evidence of the contract; and it does not follow that a party who is not a party to the contract may not be able to sue on it, if the property in the goods passes to him upon or by reason of the consignment."

This principle means that as between the original shipper and the carrier, the bill is merely evidence of their agreement. If other evidence establishes different terms were agreed, that evidence may prevail over what the bill states. The shipper might show that oral arrangements, booking confirmations, or course of dealing established terms different from those printed in the bill.

6.2.2 The Bill as Contract for Third Party Transferees

The position changes dramatically when the bill of lading is transferred to a third party. The third party was not present when the original contract was formed and has no knowledge of what might have been orally agreed. For the third party, the bill of lading itself is the contract.

This principle was established in *Leduc v Ward* [14], where Lord Esher MR stated:

"The bill of lading is signed by the master...It is a contract which binds the master and therefore the shipowner...When the indorsee of the bill of lading sues the shipowner, in my opinion he is not suing upon a contract which the law implies from previous dealings; he is suing upon a contract contained in the bill of lading."

This rule is essential to the negotiability of bills of lading. If third party buyers could be bound by oral terms not appearing in the bill, or by booking arrangements they knew nothing about, bills could not function as

---

[13] [1951] 1 KB 55
[14] (1888) 20 QBD 475

documents of title. The security of international trade requires that transferees can rely on the bill as containing the complete contract terms.

Australian law recognises this distinction clearly.

Section 11 of the *Carriage of Goods by Sea Act 1991 (Cth)* transfers rights of suit to the lawful holder of a bill of lading "as if the person had been a party to that contract." The "contract" referred to is the contract evidenced by the bill, not some separate oral or written contract that might exist between the original parties.

6.2.3 Implications of the Distinction

The distinction between the bill as evidence (for original parties) and the bill as contract (for transferees) creates a two-tier system. Shippers may be able to prove that the actual agreement differed from the bill's terms, while transferees are bound by the bill as written.

This can lead to different outcomes in litigation. If a shipper sues the carrier, the shipper might introduce evidence of oral arrangements or booking terms that modify the bill. If a subsequent buyer sues for the same cargo damage, that buyer is confined to the bill's terms and cannot benefit from oral arrangements made between shipper and carrier.

Carriers must therefore carefully ensure that bills accurately reflect what was agreed with shippers. If bills are issued containing terms different from the actual agreement, carriers face the risk that shippers will prove the actual terms, while transferees will hold carriers to the bill's terms. Consistency between oral arrangements, booking confirmations, and bill of lading terms is essential.

6.3 Terms Contained in Bills of Lading

6.3.1 Express Terms on the Face

Bills of lading contain terms in multiple locations. The face of the bill typically includes:

- Names of shipper, carrier, and consignee or party to be notified
- Description of goods, including marks, quantity, and condition

- Vessel name and voyage details
- Ports of loading and discharge
- Freight charges and payment terms
- Number of originals issued.
- Date and place of issue.
- Signature and identification of issuing party

These front-page details establish the basic parameters of the carriage contract. They identify who is carrying what goods, from where to where, on which vessel, and for what freight. While much of this is factual information serving the receipt function, it also forms part of the contract by defining the carrier's obligations.

6.3.2 Standard Terms on the Reverse or Incorporated Documents

The detailed contractual terms typically appear on the reverse side of the bill or in a separate document incorporated by reference.

These terms address:

- The carrier's obligations regarding care of goods
- Exceptions from liability (perils of the sea, acts of God, etc.)
- Limitation of liability amounts and calculation methods
- Time limits for bringing claims.
- Jurisdiction and applicable law clauses
- General average and salvage provisions
- Paramount clauses incorporating international conventions.
- Freight payment terms and lien rights
- Himalaya clauses extending protections to servants and contractors.
- Both-to-blame collision clauses
- General provisions on deck cargo, dangerous goods, delays, etc.

These terms may run to several pages of dense legal text. In liner shipping, they are standardised across the carrier's fleet and operations. Individual shippers typically have no ability to negotiate these terms; They are offered on a take-it-or-leave-it basis.

6.3.3 Incorporation by Reference

Bills of lading frequently state that certain terms are incorporated by reference to other documents. A common example is: "All terms, conditions and exceptions as per standard terms and conditions available at www.carrier.com." Another variant: "Freight and all other conditions as per carrier's published tariff."

For incorporation by reference to be effective, several requirements must be met. First, the reference must be sufficiently clear and specific. Vague references to "usual terms" or "standard conditions" may be ineffective if the incorporated terms cannot be identified. Second, the incorporated terms must be accessible to the other party. If terms are contained in documents not provided to the shipper, incorporation may fail.

Third, the incorporating language must be adequate to bring the specific terms into the contract. General references may not incorporate specific or unusual terms, particularly those that are onerous or unusual. The more unusual or unexpected a term is, the more clearly it must be drawn to the other party's attention for effective incorporation.

Australian courts apply these principles consistently. In *Interfoto Picture Library Ltd v Stiletto Visual Programmes Ltd* [15], an English case followed in Australia, the court held that particularly onerous or unusual terms must be fairly and reasonably brought to the other party's attention. General incorporation language may not suffice for such terms.

6.3.4 Paramount Clauses

A paramount clause is a clause in a bill of lading that expressly incorporates one of the international carriage conventions (*Hague, Hague-Visby, Hamburg, or Rotterdam Rules*). A typical paramount clause reads:

"The Hague-Visby Rules as enacted in the country of shipment shall apply to this contract."

Paramount clauses serve to clarify which legal regime applies to the carriage. This is important because different jurisdictions may apply different versions of the rules, and parties may contract for application of rules that would not otherwise mandatorily apply.

---

[15] [1989] QB 433

However, in Australian law, the paramountcy of the *Hague-Visby Rules* is established by statute rather than contract. Section 9 of the *Carriage of Goods by Sea Act 1991 (Cth)* provides that the *Hague-Visby Rules* "have the force of law in relation to carriage of goods by sea" between Australian ports and foreign ports. The Rules apply mandatorily regardless of what the bill of lading says.

A paramount clause in a bill of lading for Australian trade might specify which version applies (such as the *SDR Protocol* version) or might purport to apply different rules (such as the *Hamburg Rules*). However, such clauses cannot override the mandatory application of *the Hague-Visby Rules* under the Australian Act.

The statutory regime prevails over contractual choice.

6.3.5 Clause Construction Principles

When interpreting terms in bills of lading, Australian courts apply standard contractual interpretation principles, with some modifications reflecting the commercial nature and international character of shipping contracts.

The primary rule is that courts seek to ascertain the objective intention of the parties from the language used, considered in its commercial context. Technical or legalistic interpretations that produce uncommercial results are avoided. The contract is read as a whole, with individual clauses construed in context rather than in isolation.

Ambiguities are resolved using the *contra proferentem* rule against the party who drafted the clause. Since carriers draft bills of lading on a standard form basis, ambiguities are typically resolved against the carrier and in favour of cargo interests. This rule applies with particular force to exemption and limitation clauses, which must be clearly drafted to be effective.

Courts also apply the principle that specific clauses prevail over general ones. If a bill contains both a general term and a specific term addressing the same subject, the specific term controls. Similarly, handwritten or typed terms prevail over pre-printed terms where they conflict, as handwritten terms reflect the parties' specific agreement for this particular shipment.

6.4 Incorporation of Charterparty Terms

6.4.1 The Problem of Incorporation

One of the most complex and litigated areas of shipping law concerns the incorporation of charterparty terms into bills of lading. The issue arises when a vessel is chartered and bills of lading are issued either by the shipowner or the charterer. The charterparty contains detailed terms governing the relationship between owner and charterer. The question is whether and to what extent those charterparty terms also govern the relationship between the carrier and holders of bills of lading.

The problem is acute because third party holders of bills have no knowledge of the charterparty and no opportunity to negotiate its terms. If charterparty terms are incorporated into bills, transferees may be bound by terms they have never seen and could not reasonably have anticipated. Yet without incorporation, the shipowner issuing bills under a charterparty may face inconsistent obligations under the charterparty and under the bills.

The law has struggled to balance these competing concerns, resulting in a complex body of case law establishing when and how charterparty terms are incorporated into bills of lading. The Australian position follows English authorities closely, with the High Court and Federal Court having addressed these issues in several significant decisions.

6.4.2 General Principles of Incorporation

For charterparty terms to be incorporated into a bill of lading, the bill must contain language purporting to incorporate them. General words such as "all terms and conditions of the charterparty dated [date]" or "freight and other conditions as per charterparty" are commonly used.

However, courts apply a restrictive approach to incorporation. Not all charterparty terms are incorporated, even when general words are used.

The courts distinguish between different types of terms:

1. Directly germane terms

Terms that directly relate to the shipment and delivery of cargo are readily incorporated. These include terms about freight, laytime, demurrage, discharge arrangements, and similar matters directly relevant to cargo operations.

2. Collateral or ancillary terms

Terms that relate to the relationship between shipowner and charterer but not directly to cargo operations are less likely to be incorporated. These include arbitration clauses, jurisdiction clauses, cesser clauses, and similar provisions.

3. Repugnant terms

Terms that would contradict or be inconsistent with the bill of lading itself cannot be incorporated. For example, a charterparty term making the charterer responsible for loading costs cannot be incorporated into a bill issued to a third party who has no connection to the charter.

This framework was established in T.*W. Thomas & Co Ltd v Portsea Steamship Co Ltd* [16], a House of Lords decision followed in Australia. The case involved a bill with an incorporation clause referring to "all the terms and conditions" of the charterparty. The court held this did not incorporate an arbitration clause because such clauses are not directly relevant to cargo operations.

6.4.3 Incorporation of Arbitration Clauses

Arbitration clauses in charterparties are a particular focus of litigation. Shipowners often prefer arbitration over court litigation, and charterparties routinely contain arbitration clauses. The question is whether general words of incorporation bring the arbitration clause into bills of lading issued under the charter.

The English rule, established in *Thomas v Portsea* and confirmed in *The Varenna* [17], is that general words of incorporation do not incorporate arbitration clauses unless the incorporating language specifically refers to arbitration. General phrases like "all terms and conditions" are insufficient.

---

[16] [1912] AC 1
[17] [1984] QB 599

The bill must state something like "including arbitration clause" or "all terms including dispute resolution."

Australian law follows this approach. In Carrington Slipways Pty Ltd v Patrick Operations Pty Ltd [18], the New South Wales Court of Appeal held that an arbitration clause in a charterparty was not incorporated into bills of lading by general words. The court emphasised that arbitration clauses are procedural rather than substantive, and general incorporation language does not extend to such clauses.

The policy behind this rule is protection of third-party bill holders. A buyer who purchases goods and receives a bill of lading does not expect to be required to arbitrate in a foreign jurisdiction under procedures specified in a charterparty they have never seen. Unless the bill specifically alerts them to arbitration requirements, they should not be bound.

However, specific words do incorporate arbitration. If a bill states *"freight, demurrage and all other conditions including the arbitration clause as per charterparty dated [date],"* the arbitration clause is incorporated. The requirement is for specific reference to arbitration, making clear to bill holders that disputes must be arbitrated.

6.4.4 Incorporation of Jurisdiction and Choice of Law Clauses

Similar principles apply to jurisdiction and choice of law clauses. These are viewed as procedural provisions ancillary to the main cargo obligations. General incorporation language typically does not bring them into the bill of lading contract.

The leading Australian authority is *Mauritius Oil Refineries Ltd v Stolt-Nielsen Nederland BV* [19], where the Federal Court examined whether a jurisdiction clause in a charterparty was incorporated into bills of lading. The bills contained general words stating "*all terms, conditions and exceptions of the Charterparty...are herewith incorporated.*"

The court held the jurisdiction clause was not incorporated. Allsop J (as he then was) stated:

---

[18] (1991) 24 NSWLR 745

[19] (2004) 140 FCR 518

"Words of general incorporation will not incorporate into the bill of lading contract a dispute resolution clause unless the language of incorporation can fairly be read as apt to incorporate the dispute resolution clause in question having regard to its nature and language."

This restrictive approach protects bill holders from being subjected to unfamiliar forums or laws.

A holder who takes a bill in Australia should not unknowingly be subjected to exclusive jurisdiction in London or arbitration in New York merely because such clauses appear in a charterparty they have never seen.

6.4.5 Incorporation of Exemption and Limitation Clauses

Exemption clauses (which exclude or limit the carrier's liability) are more readily incorporated from charterparties into bills of lading. These clauses are viewed as directly germane to cargo operations and the carrier's obligations regarding goods.

However, the incorporation must still be clear and the clause must be apt for incorporation. If a charterparty exemption clause is drafted in language specific to the owner-charterer relationship, it may not be appropriate for incorporation into bills issued to third parties.

Australian courts examine whether incorporated exemption clauses are consistent with the mandatory provisions of the *Hague-Visby Rules*. Under section 9 of the *Carriage of Goods by Sea Act 1991 (Cth)*, the Rules apply to bills of lading issued under charterparties when those bills come into the hands of third parties. Any incorporated charterparty terms that purport to reduce the carrier's obligations below the Rules' minimum standards are void.

In *El Greco (Australia) Pty Ltd v Mediterranean Shipping Co SA* [20], the Federal Court examined bills of lading containing general words incorporating charterparty terms. The court held that while freight and demurrage provisions could be incorporated, any attempted incorporation of terms inconsistent with the Hague-Visby Rules was ineffective once the bill passed to third parties.

---

[20] [2004] FCA 202

6.4.6 Which Charterparty is Incorporated?

A practical difficulty arises when bills of lading refer to "the charterparty" without specifying which one.

A vessel may operate under multiple charters - a head charter between the owner and a time charterer, and a sub-charter between the time charterer and a voyage charterer. Bills might be issued under either charter. Which charterparty's terms are incorporated?

Courts have held that the relevant charterparty is the one under which the bill was actually issued.

This is a question of fact, determined by examining who issued the bill and in what capacity. If a time charterer issues bills under a voyage charter, the voyage charter terms are incorporated, not the time charter.

However, if the bill does not identify which charterparty is relevant, incorporation may fail for uncertainty. The holder of the bill cannot be expected to investigate the ship's charter arrangements to determine which charterparty terms govern. Clear identification of the relevant charterparty is essential for effective incorporation.

6.4.7 Verbal Manipulation and Sensible Adaptation

When charterparty terms are incorporated into bills of lading, they must often be adapted to make sense in the new context. A charterparty term referring to "the charterer" might need to be read as "the shipper" or "the bill of lading holder" when incorporated into a bill.

Courts apply a principle of "sensible commercial adaptation" or "verbal manipulation" to make incorporated terms work in their new context. In *The Varenna* [21], the court stated that words may be "adapted" to make grammatical and commercial sense when terms are incorporated from one document to another.

---

[21] [1984] QB 599

However, this adaptation has limits. Courts will not rewrite terms or change their fundamental character. If a term cannot sensibly be applied to bill of lading holders even with reasonable adaptation, it is not incorporated despite general incorporating language.

Australian courts apply this principle cautiously.

In *Hi-Fert Pty Ltd v Kiukiang Maritime Carriers Inc (No 5)* [22], the Federal Court considered how charterparty clauses should be adapted when incorporated into bills. The court emphasised that adaptation must be reasonable and must not fundamentally alter the term's character or effect.

6.5 The Hague-Visby Rules and Freedom of Contract

6.5.1 Mandatory Application of the Rules

A fundamental principle of Australian shipping law is that the *Hague-Visby Rules*, as enacted in Schedule 1A to the *Carriage of Goods by Sea Act 1991 (Cth)*, apply mandatorily to contracts of carriage evidenced by bills of lading.

Section 9(1) provides that the Rules "have the force of law" in relation to specified carriage.

The mandatory application means parties cannot contract out of the Rules' provisions. Article III rule 8 of the *Hague-Visby Rules* expressly states: "Any clause, covenant, or agreement in a contract of carriage relieving the carrier or the ship from liability...or lessening such liability otherwise than as provided in these Rules, shall be null and void and of no effect."

This prohibition ensures minimum standards of carrier liability. No matter what the bill of lading or charterparty says, the carrier cannot reduce obligations below the Rules' minimum. The carrier must exercise due diligence to make the vessel seaworthy, properly care for cargo, and cannot rely on exceptions beyond those specified in Article IV rule 2.

6.5.2 Terms That Increase Carrier Liability

---

[22] (1998) 90 FCR 1

While the Rules set a floor for carrier liability, they do not prevent carriers and cargo interests from agreeing to higher standards. Article V of the _Hague-Visby Rules_ states:

"A carrier shall be at liberty to surrender in whole or in part all or any of his rights and immunities or to increase any of his responsibilities and liabilities under these Rules."

Parties may therefore agree that the carrier will have greater liability than the Rules require. For example, they might agree to unlimited liability rather than the per-package limitation, or might agree that the carrier is absolutely liable for cargo loss without the benefit of the Article IV rule 2 exceptions.

Such agreements are valid and enforceable. However, they must be clearly expressed. Courts do not readily imply that carriers have agreed to greater liability than required. If a bill contains terms that appear to increase liability, courts examine whether the parties clearly intended that result or whether the terms can be reconciled with the Rules' standard liability.

6.5.3 The Relationship Between Bill of Lading Terms and the Rules

Bills of lading may contain terms that appear to conflict with the _Hague-Visby Rules._ For example, a bill might include broad exemption clauses purporting to relieve the carrier from liability in circumstances not covered by Article IV rule 2. How are such conflicts resolved?

The answer is that the Rules prevail. Section 9 of the _Carriage of Goods by Sea Act 1991 (Cth)_ gives the Rules "the force of law." Contractual terms inconsistent with the Rules are void under Article III rule 8. Courts apply the Rules and disregard conflicting contractual provisions.

However, courts attempt to construe bills of lading harmoniously with the Rules where possible. If a clause can be interpreted consistently with the Rules, that interpretation is preferred over one that would create a conflict. The presumption is that parties intended to comply with the law, not to include invalid terms.

In *Shipping Corporation of India Ltd v Gamlen Chemical Co (A/Asia) Pty Ltd* [23], the High Court of Australia examined the relationship between bill of lading terms and the Rules (then the Hague Rules). The court emphasised that the Rules establish minimum standards that cannot be contracted away, and that bill terms must be read subject to that constraint.

6.5.4 Excluding or Limiting the Rules' Application

The *Hague-Visby Rules* apply to bills of lading covering carriage from or to Australian ports. Section 9(2) of the *Carriage of Goods by Sea Act 1991 (Cth)* provides that the Rules do not apply to charterparties, but section 9(3) clarifies that they do apply to bills of lading issued pursuant to a charterparty:

"from the moment at which such bill of lading regulates the relations between a carrier and a holder of the same who is not the charterer."

This means charterers dealing directly with shipowners under charterparties do not get the benefit of the Rules. However, when a bill of lading issued under a charterparty is transferred to a third party, the Rules apply to protect that third party.

Parties sometimes attempt to exclude the Rules' application by contractual stipulations. For example, a bill might state "This contract is not subject to any international convention." Such clauses are ineffective. The Rules apply by force of statute, and contractual attempts to exclude them are void.

6.5.5 Choice of Law and the Rules

Bills of lading often contain choice of law clauses selecting a particular country's law to govern the contract. Such clauses are generally effective for matters not covered by the *Hague-Visby Rules*. However, they cannot displace the mandatory application of the Rules to carriage within their scope.

If a bill of lading for carriage from Melbourne to Hamburg states "This contract shall be governed by Japanese law," the choice of law clause applies to matters not addressed by the *Hague-Visby Rules* (such as formation, interpretation, remedies beyond the Rules' scope). However, the *Hague-Visby Rules* as enacted in the *Carriage of Goods by Sea Act 1991 (Cth)* still apply

---

[23] (1980) 147 CLR 142

mandatorily to the carrier's obligations regarding cargo care, exceptions, and limitation.

This principle was confirmed in *The Hollandia* [24], a House of Lords decision followed in Australia.

A bill of lading contained a choice of Dutch law clause that would have subjected the contract to lower limitation amounts than the *Hague-Visby Rules* provided. The court held the choice of law clause could not override the mandatory application of the *Hague-Visby Rules* under English legislation equivalent to the Australian Act.

6.6 Standard Terms and Conditions in Liner Bills

6.6.1 Industry Standard Forms

Liner operators typically use standardised bill of lading forms developed by industry bodies or law firms. Common forms include:

- CONLINEBILL 2000 (Conference Liner Bill)
- CONGENBILL (General Purpose Bill)
- MULTIDOC 95 (Multimodal Transport Bill)
- Carrier-specific forms based on these models.

These forms represent industry consensus on appropriate terms for liner carriage. They incorporate the *Hague-Visby Rules* (or whichever rules apply in the relevant jurisdiction), include standard exception and limitation clauses, and address common issues like freight, demurrage, jurisdiction, and general average.

The advantage of standard forms is predictability. Shippers, banks, insurers, and cargo interests become familiar with the terms. Legal issues have been tested in courts, creating precedent. Transactions proceed smoothly because parties understand what the terms mean.

However, standard forms also present challenges. They are drafted by or for carriers and naturally favour carrier interests within the bounds of mandatory law. Individual shippers typically cannot negotiate terms. The dense legal

[24] [1983] 1 AC 565

language may not be fully understood by shippers, particularly small businesses or those unfamiliar with shipping.

6.6.2 Common Clause Types in Liner Bills

Liner bills of lading typically contain:

a. ***Paramount Clause*** - Incorporating the applicable international convention (Hague-Visby Rules in Australian trades).

b. ***Carrier's Responsibility Clause*** - Defining the carrier's obligations regarding cargo care, often tracking Article III rule 2 of the Hague-Visby Rules.

c. ***Exceptions Clause*** - Listing circumstances where the carrier is not liable, incorporating Article IV rule 2 exceptions and sometimes adding others subject to the Rules' constraints.

d. ***Limitation Clause*** - Establishing per-package or per-kilo limitations as permitted by Article IV rule 5 of the Hague-Visby Rules.

e. ***Freight Clause*** - Specifying freight rates, payment terms, and the carrier's lien over goods for unpaid freight.

f. ***Both-to-Blame Collision Clause*** - Providing that if the ship collides with another vessel and cargo owners recover from the other vessel, they must indemnify the carrier "designed to address quirks of U.S. collision law.

g. ***General Average and Salvage Clause*** - Requiring cargo interests to contribute to general average and salvage expenses in accordance with York-Antwerp Rules.

h. ***Himalaya Clause*** - Extending the carrier's protections and limitations to servants, agents, and independent contractors involved in the carriage.

i. ***Time Bar Clause*** - Requiring claims to be brought within specified time periods, typically one year as provided in Article III rule 6 of the Hague-Visby Rules.

j. ***Jurisdiction and Arbitration Clause*** - Specifying where disputes must be litigated or arbitrated.

k. ***Notification Clause*** - Requiring notice of loss or damage within specified times after delivery.

l. ***Deck Cargo Clause*** - Permitting carriage on deck (particularly for containers) and excluding liability for deck cargo beyond the Rules' requirements.

m. ***Dangerous Goods Clause*** - Imposing obligations on shippers regarding declaration of dangerous goods and permitting the carrier to dispose of undeclared dangerous goods.

Each of these clauses serves specific purposes and raises distinct legal issues. Understanding their operation requires careful analysis of their interaction with the Hague-Visby Rules and other mandatory law.

6.6.3 Himalaya Clauses

Himalaya clauses deserve special attention because they address a significant gap in the Hague-Visby Rules. The Rules limit the carrier's liability, but what about independent contractors, stevedores, terminal operators, and other parties who handle cargo?

At common law, cargo owners might sue such parties in tort, avoiding the carrier's contractual limitations. To prevent this, carriers include Himalaya clauses extending the bill of lading's protections to third parties involved in the carriage.

A typical Himalaya clause states: "Every servant, agent, or independent contractor of the carrier shall have the benefit of all exemptions and limitations of liability contained in this bill of lading. For this purpose, the carrier is or shall be deemed to be acting as agent or trustee for such persons, and such persons shall be deemed to be parties to the contract evidenced by this bill of lading."

The effectiveness of Himalaya clauses was confirmed in *Scruttons Ltd v Midland Silicones Ltd* [25] and *The Eurymedon* [26], English cases followed in Australia. These cases established that despite the privity of contract doctrine, third parties can claim the benefit of Himalaya clauses through agency or trust mechanisms.

Australian law has developed this area through both case law and statute. The *Civil Liability (Third Party Claims Against Insurers) Act 2017 (Cth)* and equivalent State legislation provide frameworks for third party claims. Himalaya clauses remain important in ensuring consistent treatment of all parties involved in cargo operations.

6.6.4 Electronic Commerce Clauses

Modern liner bills increasingly include clauses addressing electronic communications and documentation. These clauses may:

- Authorise use of electronic bills of lading where available.
- Permit electronic notifications and communications.
- Address electronic data interchange (EDI) for freight and customs documentation.
- Specify rules for digital signatures and authentication.

Such clauses facilitate the digitalisation of shipping documentation while providing legal frameworks for electronic operations. They complement the Electronic Transactions Act 1999 (Cth) by establishing contractual agreement to use electronic methods.

6.7 Unfair Contract Terms and Consumer Protection

6.7.1 The Australian Consumer Law

The *Australian Consumer Law (ACL)*, contained in Schedule 2 to the *Competition and Consumer Act 2010 (Cth)*, includes provisions addressing unfair terms in consumer contracts and small business contracts. These

---

[25] [1962] AC 446
[26] [1975] AC 154

provisions potentially apply to some bill of lading contracts, though most commercial shipping falls outside their scope.

Part 2-3 of the ACL provides that a term of a consumer contract is void if it is unfair and the contract is a standard form contract. A term is unfair if it would cause significant imbalance in the parties' rights and obligations, is not reasonably necessary to protect the legitimate interests of the party advantaged by the term, and would cause detriment to a party if relied upon.

The ACL's unfair terms provisions have limited application to shipping because most shippers are businesses rather than consumers, and the ACL's small business protections only apply to contracts where the upfront price does not exceed specified thresholds (currently $300,000 or $1,000,000 depending on contract length).

6.7.2 Potential Application to Shipping Contracts

Where shippers are consumers (for example, individuals shipping personal effects internationally) or small businesses entering modest value contracts, the ACL's unfair terms provisions might apply. Terms in bills of lading that might be challenged as unfair include:

- Broad exemption clauses that go beyond what the Hague-Visby Rules permit
- Onerous jurisdiction or arbitration clauses requiring disputes in distant forums.
- Unilateral variation clauses allowing carriers to change terms.
- Penalty clauses imposing excessive charges for minor breaches.
- Terms imposing liability on shippers without fault.

However, many shipping terms would likely be held "reasonably necessary" to protect carriers' legitimate interests, particularly given the international nature of shipping, the substantial risks carriers face, and the need for standardisation across the industry. The interaction between the ACL and shipping law remains relatively undeveloped in Australian jurisprudence.

6.7.3 Exclusion of Statutory Guarantees

The ACL also implies certain guarantees into contracts for the supply of services, including that services will be rendered with due care and skill.

Section 64A of the ACL permits contracting out of these guarantees for certain transport contracts, but with limitations.

Carriers cannot exclude the statutory guarantees for carriage of passengers or their baggage.

For carriage of goods, exclusion may be possible but only to the extent permitted by other legislation such as the *Carriage of Goods by Sea Act 1991 (Cth).* This means the *Hague-Visby Rules'* limitations on carrier liability are effective, but attempts to reduce liability below those rules would violate both the *Hague-Visby Rules* and potentially the *ACL.*

6.8 Interpretation Issues and Common Disputes

6.8.1 Inconsistency Between Different Terms

Bills of lading sometimes contain terms that appear inconsistent with each other. For example, the face of the bill might state "freight prepaid" while terms on the reverse preserve the carrier's lien for unpaid freight. Or a Himalaya clause might purport to extend protections to third parties while another clause states the carrier alone is liable.

Courts resolve such inconsistencies by applying established interpretation principles. Specific terms prevail over general ones. Typed or handwritten terms prevail over printed standard terms. Terms dealing specifically with the matter at hand prevail over boilerplate provisions. The contract is read as a whole to achieve a commercially sensible result.

If an inconsistency cannot be resolved by these methods, the *contra proferentem* rule applies, and ambiguities are resolved against the carrier who drafted the bill. This rule applies forcefully to exemption and limitation clauses, which must be clearly drafted to be effective.

6.8.2 The Freight Prepaid/Collect Distinction

Bills of lading typically state whether freight is "prepaid" or "collect." This distinction has important consequences for who bears the risk of freight payment and when the carrier must deliver goods.

"Freight prepaid" means freight has been paid before or at the time of shipment. The carrier cannot refuse delivery for non-payment of freight. However, the carrier retains a lien for other charges like demurrage or detention that may arise after shipment.

"Freight collect" means freight is payable at destination before delivery. The carrier can refuse delivery until freight is paid and has a possessory lien over the goods. The consignee or bill holder must pay to obtain delivery, even if the shipper was originally responsible for freight.

Disputes arise when bills incorrectly state freight status.

If a bill states "prepaid" but freight was not actually paid, who bears the loss?

Generally, if the carrier issued the bill stating freight prepaid, the carrier cannot claim freight from the consignee or bill holder, and the carrier's remedy is against the shipper. The carrier's statement in the bill estops it from denying that freight was paid.

6.8.3 Delivery Location and Responsibility Termination

Bills of lading specify the port or place of discharge where the carrier's responsibility ends. In traditional port-to-port bills, the carrier's obligation ends when goods are discharged from the vessel at the named port. In multimodal or door-to-door bills, the carrier's responsibility may extend to inland delivery.

Disputes arise about when and where the carrier's responsibility terminates. The Hague-Visby Rules apply from loading to discharge (Article I(e)). But bills may extend the carrier's responsibility to include periods before loading or after discharge. The terms must be carefully examined to determine the scope of responsibility.

Related issues concern where delivery must occur. If a bill names a port but the vessel cannot berth there (due to congestion, strikes, or other obstacles), can the carrier deliver at a substitute location? This depends on the bill's terms and applicable law. Some bills include "port substitution" clauses permitting delivery at alternative locations in specified circumstances.

6.8.4 The Right to Delivery and Competing Claims

Bills of lading as documents of title confer the right to delivery on the lawful holder. But situations arise where multiple parties claim the same goods, perhaps due to competing sales, fraud, or documentary irregularities. How does the carrier determine who should receive delivery?

The carrier's obligation is to deliver to the person who presents the original bill of lading properly endorsed. If one person presents a valid bill, the carrier must deliver to that person, even if others claim ownership. The carrier is protected by delivering against the bill, and disputes about who actually owns the goods are for the claimants to resolve among themselves.

Problems arise when no bill is presented (perhaps because it was lost) or when competing originals appear (due to fraud or irregular documentation). Courts have held that carriers must exercise care and good faith in such situations but are not insurers against all risks. If the carrier delivers to the apparent lawful holder after reasonable inquiry, the carrier may be protected even if it later emerges that another party had better rights.

6.9 Conclusion

The bill of lading as evidence of the contract of carriage serves the essential function of defining the legal relationship between carrier and cargo interests. For the original shipper, the bill evidences the contract but may be supplemented by other evidence of the parties' agreement. For third party transferees, the bill is the contract itself, and they are bound by its terms regardless of what arrangements may have existed between shipper and carrier.

The terms contained in bills of lading must be understood in the context of the mandatory Hague-Visby Rules as implemented in Australian law. While parties have some freedom to agree on terms, they cannot reduce the carrier's responsibilities below the Rules' minimum standards. Attempts to do so are void, and courts will disregard such terms.

The incorporation of charterparty terms into bills of lading presents particular challenges, requiring careful analysis of which terms are apt for incorporation and how they must be adapted to apply to bill of lading relationships. Australian courts apply restrictive principles, particularly regarding procedural terms like arbitration and jurisdiction clauses, to protect third party bill holders from being bound by unfamiliar and unreasonable terms.

As international commerce continues to evolve, with increasing digitalisation and changing trading patterns, the contract evidence function of bills of lading adapts while maintaining its fundamental character. Understanding how bills evidence contracts, what terms they contain, and how those terms interact with mandatory law remains essential for all participants in maritime trade.

In the following chapters, we will examine the document of title function in detail (Chapter 7), specific obligations regarding delivery (Chapter 8), and the limitations and exceptions available to carriers (Chapter 9). The contractual framework established through the bill of lading, as examined in this chapter, provides the foundation for understanding these operational aspects of the carrier-cargo relationship.

Chapter 7: The Bill of Lading as Document of Title

7.1 Introduction

The characterisation of the bill of lading as a document of title is perhaps its most distinctive and commercially significant feature. This function enables goods to be bought, sold, pledged, and financed while in transit, transforming maritime commerce from a simple transportation service into a dynamic system supporting complex international trade. The document of title function allows constructive possession and delivery of goods through transfer of paper (or electronic records), making possible the rapid succession of sales that characterises commodity trading and enabling banks to provide secured financing against cargo.

This chapter examines the concept of the bill of lading as a document of title under Australian law, exploring its historical development, legal foundations, practical operation, and contemporary challenges. Understanding this function is essential because it underpins international sales, trade finance, marine insurance, and numerous other commercial activities that depend on the ability to deal with goods while they are at sea.

7.2 The Concept of Document of Title at Common Law

7.2.1 Historical Development

The recognition of bills of lading as documents of title developed gradually through mercantile custom and judicial acceptance. In early maritime trade, goods could only be dealt with through physical possession. A buyer had to wait until goods arrived to take delivery, and sellers could not transfer ownership while goods were at sea. This created significant commercial inefficiency, particularly for long-distance trades.

Merchants developed the practice of treating bills of lading as representing the goods themselves. Transfer of the bill came to be understood as transfer of the goods. By the seventeenth century, English mercantile custom recognised that endorsing and delivering a bill of lading passed constructive possession of the goods to the transferee. This custom was adopted by the common law courts.

In *Lickbarrow v Mason* [27], Lord Mansfield explicitly recognised bills of lading as documents of title, stating that the bill "is the symbol of the goods, and...the delivery of the symbol is equivalent to the delivery of the thing itself." This judicial recognition gave formal legal effect to what merchants had long practiced.

The development continued through the nineteenth century as courts elaborated the legal consequences of the document of title character. It became established that the lawful holder of a bill of lading could demand delivery from the carrier, that transfer of the bill passed constructive possession, and that (subject to the intention of parties) transfer could pass property in the goods.

7.2.2 What Makes a Document a "Document of Title"

Not every document relating to goods is a document of title. The term has a specific legal meaning. A document of title is one that, by mercantile custom and legal recognition, represents the goods themselves such that transfer of the document transfers constructive possession and (potentially) ownership of the goods.

The essential characteristics of a document of title are:

- It must be issued by or on behalf of the person in possession of the goods (the carrier or warehouseman)
- It must acknowledge receipt of specific goods.
- Transfer of the document must pass the right to receive delivery of the goods.
- The holder of the document must be able to demand delivery from the person in possession.
- The document must be recognised in trade as representing the goods.

Bills of lading satisfy all these criteria. So do warehouse receipts issued by warehousemen, and dock warrants issued by wharfingers. But ordinary receipts, delivery notes, or invoices do not, because they are not recognised as representing the goods or conferring the right to demand delivery.

---

[27] (1787) 2 TR 63

7.2.3 Constructive Possession and Symbolic Delivery

The document of title function operates through the legal concepts of constructive possession and symbolic delivery. While the goods are physically in the carrier's custody, legal possession is held by whoever lawfully holds the bill of lading. The carrier is a mere bailee holding on behalf of the bill holder.

When the bill is transferred, possession of the goods is deemed to pass to the new holder even though the goods remain on the ship. This "constructive" or "symbolic" possession is recognised for numerous legal purposes:

- Determining who can sue for conversion or damage to goods.
- Establishing who bears the risk of loss.
- Identifying who has an insurable interest.
- Ascertaining who can give good title to subsequent purchasers.

The concept of symbolic delivery is crucial to international sales.

In a CIF (Cost, Insurance, Freight) contract, the seller performs by "delivering" the goods through tendering the bill of lading and other documents. Physical delivery of the goods comes later, when the vessel arrives at destination. The buyer takes "delivery" when receiving the bill, becoming owner and bearing risk from that moment.

7.2.4 The Bill of Lading and Other Documents of Title

While bills of lading are the most important documents of title in international trade, other documents serve similar functions in different contexts. Understanding the distinctions helps clarify what makes bills of lading special.

Warehouse receipts are issued by warehousemen acknowledging storage of goods. Like bills of lading, they are negotiable documents of title. Transfer passes constructive possession and the right to demand delivery from the warehouse. They serve commodity trading, particularly for goods stored pending sale.

Dock warrants are similar to warehouse receipts but specific to goods stored at docks or wharves. They were historically important in port storage but are less common in modern containerised shipping.

Delivery orders are documents by which a person in possession of goods (carrier or warehouseman) is instructed to deliver goods to a specified person. They can represent documents of title if sufficiently certain and if recognised by mercantile custom, though their status is less clear than bills of lading.

Sea waybills are not documents of title, as discussed in Chapter 3. They evidence contracts of carriage but are not transferable and do not need to be presented for delivery. This makes them unsuitable for documentary sales or trade finance but efficient for direct shipments between related parties.

7.3 Statutory Recognition in Australia

7.3.1 The Carriage of Goods by Sea Act 1991 (Cth)

Australian law provides statutory recognition of bills of lading as documents of title through section 11 of the *Carriage of Goods by Sea Act 1991 (Cth).* While this section primarily addresses the transfer of contractual rights, it implicitly recognises the document of title function by establishing that the "lawful holder" of a bill has rights to enforce the contract of carriage.

Section 11(2) defines "lawful holder" as a person in possession of a bill of lading who has become the holder either by being identified in the bill as the person to whom delivery is to be made, or through transfer of the bill. This definition acknowledges that bills are transferable and that holders have special status regarding the goods.

Section 11(1) provides: "Where a person becomes the lawful holder of a bill of lading, there are transferred to and vested in the person by virtue of becoming the holder all rights of suit under the contract of carriage as if the person had been a party to that contract." This statutory transfer of contractual rights complements the common law recognition of the bill as conferring possessory rights.

The section addresses a historical problem where transferees of bills obtained possession of goods but not contractual rights against carriers. Before statutory intervention, transferees might be unable to sue carriers for cargo damage because they were not parties to the contract. Section 11 remedies this by transferring contractual rights along with the bill, ensuring that the document of title function is supported by enforceable contractual rights.

7.3.2 Bills of Lading Act 1855 - Historical Context

Before the *Carriage of Goods by Sea Act 1991 (Cth),* the *Bills of Lading Act 1855 (Imp)* had applied in Australia as part of imperial legislation. This Act represented the first statutory intervention to address the problem of transferring contractual rights with bills of lading.

The 1855 Act provided that consignees and endorsees of bills of lading would have "transferred to and vested in" them all rights of suit as if the contract had been made with them. This language is echoed in section 11 of the 1991 Act, showing continuity in approach.

However, the 1855 Act had limitations. It did not apply to all bills (only those where property passed upon or by reason of consignment or endorsement), and it did not clearly address sea waybills or other modern transport documents. The 1991 Act represents a more comprehensive approach, addressing a broader range of sea carriage documents and clarifying the position of various types of holders.

7.3.3 Sale of Goods Legislation

The *Sale of Goods Act 1923 (NSW)* and equivalent legislation in other Australian states contain provisions recognising the role of documents of title in passing property. Section 26 addresses the transfer of title by non-owners, providing that where goods are sold by someone with a voidable title, the buyer acquires good title if taking in good faith and without notice of the seller's defect in title.

Section 29 deals with delivery, providing that delivery to a carrier for transmission to a buyer is prima facie deemed to be delivery to the buyer. Section 30 addresses risk, stating that (unless otherwise agreed) risk passes with property. These provisions interact with the document of title function of bills of lading in international sales.

More specifically, section 32 addresses sales involving carriage by sea. It provides that unless otherwise agreed, where goods are sent by sea under circumstances in which it is usual to insure, the seller must give notice to enable the buyer to insure during sea transit. This section recognises the standard practice in CIF sales where the seller arranges insurance but the buyer bears risk during the voyage.

Section 33 addresses the transfer of bills of lading, providing that where a seller delivers a bill of lading to a buyer, the buyer obtains such property in the goods as the seller had or had power to transfer. This recognises that transfer of the bill can transfer property, though it does not automatically do so, and the intention of parties under section 18 governs when property passes.

7.3.4 Personal Property Securities Act 2009 (Cth)

The *Personal Property Securities Act 2009 (Cth)* (PPSA) establishes a comprehensive regime for security interests in personal property, including goods. The PPSA recognises documents of title in its definition of "inventory," which includes goods held for sale or lease and goods that are raw materials or work in progress.

However, the PPSA does not fundamentally change the document of title character of bills of lading. Bills continue to function as they did before the PPSA. What the PPSA does is provide a registration system for security interests, which can apply when bills are used as collateral for financing.

A bank taking a bill of lading as security for a loan may need to register its security interest on the *Personal Property Securities Register* to perfect its interest against other creditors. However, the document of title function - the ability to transfer possession and potentially ownership through transfer of the bill - operates independently of PPSA registration.

7.4 Transfer of Possession Through the Bill

7.4.1 The Mechanism of Constructive Possession

When a bill of lading is issued to a shipper, the carrier acknowledges holding goods on behalf of that shipper. The shipper has constructive possession – ie legal possession without physical custody. When the shipper transfers the bill to a buyer, constructive possession passes to the buyer. The carrier now holds on behalf of the buyer, though the carrier may not know the transfer has occurred.

This mechanism depends on the legal fiction that the bill represents the goods. Just as physical delivery of goods transfers possession, delivery of the bill transfers constructive possession. The carrier's acknowledgment of holding goods "to order" or "to the order of [named party]" creates the legal relationship necessary for constructive possession to pass with the bill.

The requirement for the bill to be negotiable (an order bill) is essential to this mechanism. Straight bills (non-negotiable bills naming a specific consignee) do not create the same constructive possession relationship. The named consignee has a right to delivery by virtue of being named, not by virtue of holding the bill. Transfer of a straight bill does not transfer constructive possession in the same way.

7.4.2 Who Can Give Good Delivery

At common law, only a person with good title can give good delivery. If a seller does not own goods, the seller cannot pass ownership to a buyer. The Latin maxim *nemo dat quod non habet* (no one can give what they do not have) expresses this principle.

However, the document of title character of bills of lading, combined with mercantile custom and statutory provisions, creates important exceptions. A person who holds a bill of lading may be able to give good title even if their own title is defective, provided the transferee takes in good faith and for value.

Section 29 of the *Sale of Goods Act 1923 (NSW)* and equivalent provisions in other states protect good faith purchasers in certain circumstances. If goods or documents of title are transferred by a person with apparent authority, a good faith transferee may acquire good title even if the transferor lacked actual authority.

The *Factors Acts* (legislation existing in Australian states before federation and still relevant in some contexts) provide that where a mercantile agent holds goods or documents of title with the owner's consent, and the agent sells or pledges the goods or documents in the ordinary course of business, the transaction is valid against the owner. This protects buyers and financiers who deal with agents holding bills of lading.

7.4.3 The Pledge of Bills of Lading

An important use of bills of lading as documents of title is in pledging them as security for loans. Banks financing international trade take bills of lading as collateral. If the borrower defaults, the bank can exercise its rights under the bill to obtain delivery and sell the goods to recover the debt.

A pledge is created by delivering the bill to the pledgee (bank) with intent to create security. The pledgee obtains special property in the goods - a possessory interest sufficient to claim delivery and sell the goods, if necessary, but not full ownership. Legal title remains with the pledgor (borrower) unless and until the pledgee exercises its power of sale.

The effectiveness of bills of lading as security depends on their document of title character. A bank holding a bill can prevent the borrower from obtaining the goods, can itself claim delivery from the carrier, and can sell the goods to a third party who will acquire good title. Without this document of title quality, bills would provide inadequate security.

Documentary credit transactions routinely involve pledges of bills of lading. The beneficiary of the credit ships goods and obtains bills, which are presented to the bank. The bank pays against the documents, taking the bills as security. When the applicant (buyer) pays or arranges payment, the bank releases the bills, allowing the buyer to claim delivery. If payment is not made, the bank can sell the goods.

7.4.4 Limitations on Constructive Possession

The constructive possession conferred by bills of lading has limits. It does not override actual physical possession in all circumstances. If goods are wrongly delivered to someone without the bill, that person obtains physical possession even though the bill holder retains constructive possession and the right to sue for wrongful delivery.

Constructive possession also does not extend to goods that have been lost or destroyed. If a ship sinks and cargo is lost, the bill no longer represents any goods. The holder has a right to sue the carrier for the loss but does not have constructive possession of anything. The bill's value shifts from representing goods to representing a claim for compensation.

Furthermore, constructive possession through a bill does not defeat statutory rights or liens that arise independently of the bill. For example, if customs authorities seise goods for violation of import restrictions, the bill holder's constructive possession does not prevent the seizure, though it may support a claim for return of goods or compensation.

7.5 Transfer of Property Through the Bill

7.5.1 Distinction Between Possession and Property

Possession and property (ownership) are distinct concepts. Transfer of a bill of lading always transfers constructive possession, but it transfers property only if the parties intend it to do so. Understanding this distinction is crucial to analysing disputes about who owns goods in transit.

A person can have possession without property (a bailee holds goods without owning them). A person can have property without possession (an owner whose goods are held by another). In many commercial transactions, possession and property are split - goods are held by carriers or warehousemen while owned by buyers or sellers.

When a bill of lading is transferred, the transferee always gets the right to claim delivery (possessory right) but gets ownership only if property has passed. Whether property passes depends on the intention of the parties to the sale, as determined by the *Sale of Goods A*ct rules and the contract terms.

7.5.2 Sale of Goods Act Rules on Passing of Property

Section 18 of the *Sale of Goods Act 1923 (NSW)* and equivalent provisions in other states contain rules for ascertaining when property passes from seller to buyer. These rules apply only where the parties have not expressed contrary intention. They are default rules.

Rule 1 provides that where there is an unconditional contract for the sale of specific goods in a deliverable state, property passes when the contract is made, regardless of when payment or delivery occurs.

Rule 2 addresses goods that need work before being deliverable, providing that property passes when the work is complete and notice given to the buyer.

Rule 3 concerns goods in a deliverable state that the seller must weigh, measure, or test to ascertain price, providing that property passes when this is done and notice given.

Rule 4 addresses goods on approval or "sale or return," providing that property passes when the buyer approves, or when the buyer does any act adopting the transaction.

Rule 5 is most relevant to international sales involving bills of lading. It addresses unascertained or future goods sold by description. Property passes when goods matching the description are unconditionally appropriated to the contract with assent of both parties.

In the context of bills of lading, Rule 5 means that property typically passes when goods are shipped and the bill of lading is issued or endorsed to the buyer. The shipment constitutes unconditional appropriation (the seller has committed those specific goods to this contract), and the buyer's prior agreement to purchase constitutes assent. Transfer of the bill evidences and effectuates this passing of property.

7.5.3 Intention in CIF and FOB Contracts

In international sales, the contract terms define when property passes. CIF (Cost, Insurance, Freight) and FOB (Free On Board) are standard international trade terms with established meanings regarding when property and risk pass.

In CIF contracts, the seller contracts to ship goods, arrange insurance, and provide documents including the bill of lading. Property and risk typically pass when the seller tenders conforming documents to the buyer, which is usually when the seller delivers the bill of lading to the buyer or to the bank in a documentary credit transaction. The buyer becomes owner while goods are at sea, bearing the risk of loss during the voyage (subject to insurance).

The CIF seller's obligation is documentary – that is to provide proper documents, not to ensure goods actually arrive. If goods are lost during the voyage, the seller still fulfills the contract by providing clean documents. The buyer must accept the documents (and pay) even if goods are lost, though the buyer can claim under the insurance.

In FOB contracts, the seller's obligation is to deliver goods on board the vessel at the port of shipment. Property and risk typically pass when goods cross the ship's rail (in traditional formulations) or when they are loaded on board (under modern Incoterms). The buyer arranges carriage and insurance from that point.

Under FOB terms, the bill of lading may be issued to the buyer's order, or the seller may take a bill and forward it to the buyer. Property passes at shipment regardless of when the bill is transferred. The bill serves primarily as evidence of shipment and to enable the buyer to claim delivery at destination.

7.5.4 Reservation of Title

Sellers sometimes wish to retain ownership of goods until payment is received, even after shipping. This can be achieved through "reservation of title" or "retention of title" clauses, combined with appropriate handling of bills of lading.

Section 20(1) of the *Sale of Goods Act 1923 (NSW)* provides: "Where there is a contract for the sale of specific goods...the seller may, by the terms of the contract or appropriation, reserve the right of disposal of the goods until certain conditions are fulfilled." This allows sellers to retain property even though goods are delivered.

In international sales, reservation of title is effectuated by the seller taking bills of lading to their own order or to the order of their agent (such as a bank). The seller retains control of the bill, meaning the buyer cannot obtain delivery until the seller releases the bill, which the seller does only upon receiving payment.

This arrangement is common in documentary credit transactions. The seller ships goods, takes a bill to the seller's order, and presents it to a bank for payment. Property remains with the seller until the bank pays (at which point property passes to the bank briefly as pledgee) and then passes to the buyer when the buyer pays the bank and receives the bill.

7.5.5 The Risk-Property Distinction

The Sale of Goods Act distinguishes between property (ownership) and risk (who bears the loss if goods are damaged or destroyed). Section 21 provides that risk prima facie passes with property, but the parties can agree otherwise.

In CIF contracts, there is a standard split between property and risk. Property passes when documents are tendered (typically after voyage commences), but risk passes at shipment when goods are loaded. The buyer therefore bears risk for a period before obtaining property. This works because the seller has arranged insurance, which covers the buyer's risk during this period.

Understanding the risk-property distinction is essential when bills of lading are lost or goods are damaged in transit. If property has passed to the buyer but goods are lost, the buyer still must pay the seller (though can claim under insurance or against the carrier). If property has not passed and goods are lost, the seller bears the loss and cannot demand payment from the buyer (though the seller can claim against carrier or insurer).

7.6 Bills of Lading in International Sales

7.6.1 The Role in CIF Contracts

CIF (Cost, Insurance, Freight) contracts are the paradigmatic international sale structure using bills of lading. The seller's obligations are:

- Contract for carriage and obtain a bill of lading.
- Insure the goods and obtain an insurance policy or certificate.
- Prepare an invoice for the price.
- Tender these documents to the buyer.

The documents are the essence of CIF performance. The seller fulfills contractual obligations by tendering conforming documents, regardless of the goods' actual condition or location. The buyer must accept and pay against conforming documents even if goods have been lost at sea (subject to claiming under insurance).

The bill of lading in a CIF sale must be:

- A shipped bill (confirming goods are on board)
- Clean (without adverse notations about condition)
- Dated within the shipment period specified in the contract.

- Covering the contract goods as described
- Properly endorsed or made out to the buyer's order.

If the bill does not meet these requirements, the buyer can reject the documents and refuse payment. The seller must provide proper documents or is in breach. This strict documentary compliance reflects the principle that in international sales, parties deal in documents representing goods rather than the physical goods themselves.

7.6.2 The Role in FOB Contracts

In FOB (Free On Board) contracts, the bill of lading plays a different but equally important role. The buyer typically arranges carriage and instructs the seller regarding vessel nomination. The bill may be issued directly to the buyer or to the buyer's agent.

The FOB seller's obligation is to deliver goods on board the nominated vessel and provide evidence of shipment. The bill of lading serves as that evidence. Once the seller obtains a bill showing goods are on board, the seller has performed and can claim payment (unless payment terms provide otherwise).

Property typically passes upon shipment in FOB contracts, not upon tender of documents. The bill therefore does not operate as the mechanism for passing property (as in CIF) but rather as evidence that property has passed and as the document enabling the buyer to claim delivery at destination.

FOB buyers must be vigilant about the bill's terms because they bear the carriage contract. If the bill contains unfavourable terms, the buyer is bound by them. Unlike CIF where the seller arranges carriage, FOB buyers effectively choose the carrier and contract terms by nominating the vessel.

7.6.3 Other Trade Terms and the Bill's Role

Modern international sales often use *Incoterms* (International Commercial Terms) published by the International Chamber of Commerce. These standard terms define the parties' obligations regarding delivery, risk, and costs. Several Incoterms involve bills of lading:

CIP *(Carriage and Insurance Paid To) is similar to CIF but applies to all modes of transport, not just* sea. The seller arranges carriage and insurance to the named destination. Bills of lading or other transport documents must be provided.

CPT (Carriage Paid To) is similar to CIP but without the insurance obligation. The seller arranges and pays for carriage, providing transport documents.

FCA (Free Carrier) involves delivery to a carrier at a specified place. The seller obtains transport documents and provides them to the buyer, though the buyer bears risk from delivery to the carrier onward.

In all these terms, transport documents (including bills of lading for sea carriage) play central roles in evidencing delivery, transferring rights, and determining when obligations are fulfilled. The document of title character enables the commercial mechanisms these trade terms contemplate.

7.6.4 Bills of Lading in Documentary Credits

Letters of credit (documentary credits) are the primary payment mechanism in international sales, and bills of lading are typically the central documents. Under a documentary credit, a bank undertakes to pay the seller upon presentation of conforming documents, including a bill of lading.

The *Uniform Customs and Practice for Documentary Credits (UCP 600)* governs most documentary credits worldwide. Article 20 of UCP 600 sets detailed requirements for bills of lading:

- Must appear to indicate the name of the carrier and be signed by the carrier or a named agent.
- Must indicate that goods have been shipped on board (for shipped bills) or provide an on board notation.
- Must indicate the port of loading and port of discharge stated in the credit.
- Must be the sole original bill of lading or full set if issued in more than one original.
- Must not indicate that goods are loaded on deck (unless the credit permits)
- Must not contain certain prohibited clauses or statements.

Banks examine bills strictly against these requirements. If a bill does not conform exactly, the bank must refuse it. This strict compliance doctrine ensures certainty in documentary credit transactions but requires precise drafting and careful attention to detail.

The document of title character of bills is essential to documentary credits. Banks take bills as security when they pay sellers. If buyers default on payment, banks can exercise rights under the bills to obtain delivery and sell goods to recover their advances. Without the document of title function, bills would provide inadequate security and documentary credits would be impractical.

7.7 The Bill of Lading and Marine Insurance

7.7.1 Insurable Interest Through the Bill

Marine cargo insurance depends on the insured having an insurable interest in the goods. An insurable interest means a legal or equitable relationship to the goods such that the insured would suffer loss if the goods were damaged or destroyed. Ownership clearly creates insurable interest, but so does holding a bill of lading.

A person holding a bill of lading has insurable interest because they have the right to claim delivery and (depending on circumstances) may have property in the goods or may bear the risk of their loss. Banks holding bills as pledgees have insurable interest because they have security interests that would be impaired if goods were lost.

The *Marine Insurance Act 1909 (Cth)* recognises various types of insurable interest. Section 10 provides that a person has insurable interest if they have any legal or equitable relation to goods at risk whereby, they may benefit from their safety or be prejudiced by their loss. Holding a bill of lading creates such interest.

7.7.2 Assignment of Insurance with the Bill

In CIF sales, sellers arrange insurance and provide buyers with insurance documents (policies or certificates). When goods are damaged or lost during the voyage, the buyer (who has acquired the goods through the bill of lading) needs to claim under the insurance.

The assignment of insurance rights accompanies the transfer of the bill of lading. Marine insurance policies typically contain terms allowing assignment, and many are issued "to order" similar to bills of lading. Transfer of the policy with the bill of lading transfers the right to claim under the insurance.

Section 57 of the *Marine Insurance Act 1909 (Cth)* provides that a marine policy is assignable unless it contains terms expressly prohibiting assignment. The assignment operates to transfer all the assignor's interest in the policy to the assignee, subject to any equities between assignor and assignee.

The practical effect is that buyers receiving bills of lading in CIF sales also receive the right to claim under insurance for loss or damage occurring during the voyage. Even if the loss occurred before the buyer acquired the bill (and thus before the buyer obtained property or bore risk), the buyer can claim as assignee of the insurance contract.

7.7.3 Warranties and the Bill's Description

Marine insurance policies contain warranties - conditions that must be strictly complied with, or the insurer is discharged from liability. Common warranties relate to the nature of goods, their packaging, the voyage route, and the vessel's seaworthiness.

The description of goods in the bill of lading is relevant to insurance warranties. If a policy insures "copper wire" and the bill of lading describes the goods as "copper wire," but delivered goods prove to be a different material, questions arise about whether the warranty was breached. If the insured misdescribed goods in the bill and the insurance, the insurer may deny coverage.

Conversely, accurate description in the bill supports insurance claims. If the bill clearly describes goods and their packaging, and loss occurs, the insured can point to the bill as evidence of what was shipped and claim that it matched the insurance description.

7.8 Problems and Limitations of the Document of Title Function

7.8.1 The Late Arrival of Documents Problem

A persistent practical problem is that bills of lading often arrive at destination after the vessel. Modern container ships are fast, while bills transmitted by courier or mail may take days. This creates pressure to deliver goods without bills, undermining the document of title function.

As discussed in Chapter 4, carriers often deliver against letters of indemnity rather than requiring presentation of bills. While commercially understandable, this practice is legally problematic. It defeats the document of title function because goods can be obtained without the document. It exposes carriers to liability for misdelivery to bill holders. It undermines the security banks have when holding bills as collateral.

The problem is particularly acute in short sea trades (such as between Australia and New Sealand) and in liner trades with efficient vessel schedules. Various solutions have been proposed:

- Express delivery of bills by courier to ensure arrival before vessels.
- Sea waybills instead of bills where negotiability is not needed.
- Electronic bills that can be transmitted almost instantaneously
- Procedures for delivery without bills backed by adequate security.

Each solution has drawbacks. Express delivery is expensive. Sea waybills eliminate the document of title function needed for sales and finance. Electronic bills face legal and practical obstacles. Delivery without bills creates liability risks. No perfect solution exists, though electronic bills offer the most promise for the future.

7.8.2 Fraud and Forgery

The value of bills of lading as documents of title makes them targets for fraud. Several types of fraud occur:

Forged bills: Fraudsters create false bills purporting to evidence shipments that never occurred, or alter genuine bills to misrepresent cargo. These forged bills may be used to obtain financing from banks or payment from buyers.

Duplicate originals: Where bills are issued in sets of originals, dishonest parties may transfer different originals to different buyers, each believing they have good title. The carrier delivers against one original, leaving other holders without goods.

Bills after goods have been delivered: Sometimes bills are transferred after the carrier has already delivered goods, perhaps against a letter of indemnity. The transferee receives a worthless document.

Misdescription: Shippers may obtain bills misdescribing goods (through letters of indemnity or complicit carriers), then use these bills to sell worthless goods as if they were valuable cargo.

Australian law provides remedies against fraud through both civil and criminal law. Persons suffering loss through fraudulent bills may sue in deceit or under the Australian Consumer Law for misleading and deceptive conduct. Criminal prosecution may be available for fraud offenses under Commonwealth or State legislation.

However, prevention is better than remedy. Banks and buyers must verify authenticity of bills, check issuing carriers' identities, and confirm shipment details independently where possible. Digital systems with secure authentication and tracking may reduce fraud opportunities.

7.8.3 Limits of Transferability in Practice

While bills of lading are theoretically negotiable, practical limits exist on transferability. Not all parties are willing to take bills, and some bills cannot effectively be transferred.

Straight bills are not fully negotiable, as discussed in Chapter 3. While they may be documents of title in a limited sense, they cannot be transferred to confer rights on new holders in the way order bills can.

Bills with restrictive endorsements may limit further transfer. If a bill is endorsed "deliver to X only" (a special endorsement), X must endorse again to transfer further, and X might refuse or be unavailable.

Bills held by banks as security are effectively non-transferable while the pledge exists. The bank holds the bill and will not release it until the borrower pays.

Time constraints may make transfer impractical. If a bill arrives shortly before the vessel, there may be insufficient time to complete additional sales and transfers before delivery must be claimed.

These practical limitations mean that while bills of lading are powerful documents of title, they are not infinitely negotiable in practice. The commercial context determines whether transfer is feasible.

7.8.4 The Inadequacy of Bills for Modern Multimodal Transport

Traditional bills of lading were developed for port-to-port sea carriage. Modern container transport often involves multimodal or door-to-door carriage, truck transport to port, sea carriage, then truck or rail delivery to final destination. Bills of lading do not perfectly fit this multimodal reality.

Multimodal transport documents attempt to address this by covering the entire journey. However, legal uncertainty exists about whether such documents are true documents of title given that they involve non-sea segments where different legal regimes apply.

The document of title concept depends on recognition by mercantile custom and law. For traditional sea bills, this recognition is long-established. For multimodal documents, recognition is less certain. Some legal systems treat them as documents of title, others do not. Banks may be hesitant to rely on them as security.

The Rotterdam Rules (not yet in force or adopted by Australia) attempt to provide a comprehensive framework for multimodal transport documents, including their negotiability and document of title character. Until such a framework is widely adopted, multimodal transport documents exist in a somewhat uncertain legal position.

7.9 Electronic Bills of Lading and the Document of Title Function

7.9.1 The Challenge of Replicating Document of Title in Electronic Form

The document of title function depends on physical possession of a tangible document. Transfer occurs through endorsement and delivery of paper. Exclusive control over the physical bill gives the holder exclusive rights to the goods. How can this be replicated electronically?

The challenge is creating a unique electronic record that can be possessed and transferred in ways analogous to physical possession and transfer of paper. The electronic record must be:

- Unique (not copiable in the way computer files normally are)
- Transferable (movable from one person to another)
- Exclusive (only one person can "hold" it at a time)
- Verifiable (authenticity and chain of transfers can be confirmed)

7.9.2 Technical Solutions: Registry and Blockchain Models

Two primary technical approaches have emerged to create electronic documents of title:

Registry models (used by systems like Bolero and essDOCS) maintain a central registry recording the current holder of each electronic bill. Transfer occurs by updating the registry to show a new holder. Only the person registered as holder can exercise rights under the bill. The registry ensures uniqueness and exclusivity.

Blockchain models (used by systems like WAVE, CargoX, and TradeLens) use distributed ledger technology to create unique digital tokens representing bills. Blockchain's immutability and consensus mechanisms ensure that tokens cannot be duplicated and transfers are reliably recorded. Possession of the private key controlling a token constitutes "holding" the electronic bill.

Both approaches can technically replicate the document of title function. The registry model is centralised, requiring trust in the registry operator but providing clear certainty about who holds each bill. The blockchain model is decentralised, removing the need to trust a central operator but requiring technical infrastructure and expertise.

7.9.3 Legal Recognition Under Australian Law

The legal status of electronic bills of lading as documents of title in Australia remains somewhat uncertain. The *Electronic Transactions Act 1999 (Cth)* provides general recognition of electronic communications and signatures but does not specifically address documents of title.

Section 11 of the _Carriage of Goods by Sea Act 1991 (Cth)_ refers to "bills of lading" without specifying that they must be in paper form. The term "lawful holder" might potentially be interpreted to include a person with electronic control of an electronic bill, though this would require judicial interpretation or legislative clarification.

The strongest argument for recognising electronic bills as documents of title in Australia is functional equivalence; if an electronic system replicates all the functions of paper bills (receipt, contract evidence, and document of title), and all parties agree to use it, courts should recognise it as effective. The _Electronic Transactions Act_ supports this approach by providing that legal requirements for documents can be satisfied by electronic communications if the information is accessible for subsequent reference.

However, explicit legislative recognition would provide greater certainty. _The Rotterdam Rules'_ provisions on electronic transport records offer a model. If Australia were to adopt similar provisions (whether through ratifying Rotterdam or through domestic legislation), electronic bills would have clear legal status.

7.9.4 Practical Barriers to Adoption

Despite technical feasibility, electronic bills face practical barriers:

Limited participation: Electronic bill systems require all parties in the shipping chain (carriers, shippers, banks, insurers, customs, ports) to participate in the same system. If any party cannot or will not use the system, paper documents must be used as a fallback.

Multiple competing systems: Several electronic bill platforms exist, each with different technical approaches and participation requirements. Lack of interoperability means parties must join multiple systems or use paper for transactions involving parties on different systems.

Banking practice: Banks, particularly smaller banks and those in developing countries, often lack systems for handling electronic bills and prefer paper documents they understand. Documentary credit practice, though theoretically accommodating electronic documents, remains paper-centric in most trades.

Legal uncertainty: Lack of clear legal recognition in many jurisdictions creates hesitation. Banks and traders want certainty that electronic bills will be recognised by courts and enforceable against carriers and other parties.

Cost and complexity: Implementing electronic systems requires investment in technology, training, and process changes. For many shippers and carriers, the benefits do not yet outweigh the costs.

Despite these barriers, momentum is building toward electronic bills. Major carriers have adopted or are testing electronic systems. Industry bodies promote digitalisation. The COVID-19 pandemic accelerated digital transformation. Electronic bills likely represent the future, though full adoption may take years.

7.10 Conclusion

The document of title function is what makes bills of lading unique and commercially indispensable. Through this function, goods can be bought, sold, and financed while in transit, enabling the rapid movement of goods and capital that characterises modern international trade. The ability to transfer constructive possession and potentially property through transfer of a document has no real equivalent in other areas of commercial law.

Understanding the document of title function requires appreciating both its common law foundations and its statutory recognition in Australia. The Carriage of Goods by Sea Act 1991 (Cth) and related legislation provide frameworks supporting the function, particularly by ensuring that holders of bills obtain enforceable contractual rights against carriers.

The function operates seamlessly in traditional international sales using CIF or FOB terms. It enables documentary credit transactions by giving banks security. It supports marine insurance by creating insurable interests. Yet it also faces challenges in modern shipping - the late arrival of documents, the rise of multimodal transport, and the need for digitalisation.

Electronic bills of lading promise to address some challenges by enabling instant transmission and maintaining security through technology. However, full realisation of electronic bills requires overcoming legal, practical, and cultural barriers. The document of title function will undoubtedly evolve, but its essential character - enabling dealings with goods through dealings with documents seems likely to persist.

In subsequent chapters, we examine the carrier's obligations regarding delivery (Chapter 8), which implement the practical side of the document of title function, and the limitations on carrier liability (Chapter 9), which define the risks inherent in treating bills as representing goods. The document of title function, as explored in this chapter, provides the commercial foundation on which these operational and liability rules build.

Chapter 8: Delivery Against Bills of Lading

8.1 Introduction

The carrier's obligation to deliver goods against presentation of the bill of lading is fundamental to the entire system of bills as documents of title.

This delivery obligation implements the practical operation of the document of title function; the holder of the bill can demand delivery, and only the holder should receive delivery. Yet delivery presents numerous challenges in modern shipping practice. Vessels arrive before documents, consignees cannot be located, goods are perishable, and commercial pressure demands swift release of cargo.

This chapter examines the legal principles governing delivery under Australian law, the practical problems that arise, and how carriers should navigate these challenges.

Understanding delivery obligations is essential because misdelivery - delivering goods without proper presentation of the bill - is one of the most serious breaches a carrier can commit. It defeats the document of title function, exposes carriers to substantial liability, and undermines the security of international trade. Yet carriers face competing pressures: the need to move cargo quickly, demands from consignees for immediate release, and practical difficulties when documentation is delayed or irregular.

8.2 The Carrier's Fundamental Delivery Obligation

8.2.1 Delivery Only Against the Bill

The cardinal rule is that carriers must deliver goods only to the person who presents an original bill of lading, properly endorsed if necessary. This obligation is implicit in the definition of a bill of lading. Section 11 of the *Carriage of Goods by Sea Act 1991 (Cth)* defines a bill as a document "by which the carrier undertakes to deliver the goods against surrender of the document."

The requirement to deliver against the bill serves multiple purposes. It protects the carrier by providing clear evidence of who is entitled to receive goods. The carrier delivers to the bill holder and is discharged. It protects cargo interests by ensuring goods go to the rightful owner - only the person with the bill can claim delivery. It supports the negotiability of bills by making the document the key to obtaining goods.

At common law, this obligation is strict. The carrier cannot deliver to someone merely because they appear to be the owner or because they have other documents (like invoices or letters of authority).

The bill of lading is the document of title, and only its presentation justifies delivery. As Lord Denning stated in *Sze Hai Tong Bank Ltd v Rambler Cycle Co Ltd* [28]:

"It is perfectly clear law that a shipowner who delivers without production of the bill of lading does so at his peril."

8.2.2 Verifying the Presenter's Entitlement

When someone presents a bill of lading, the carrier must verify their entitlement. For order bills, this requires examining the endorsement chain. The carrier checks that endorsements are complete from the original shipper through to the presenter. Each endorsement should be signed, and if special endorsements are used (naming specific endorsees), the chain must connect to the current presenter.

The carrier must also verify the presenter's identity to ensure they are the person named in the last endorsement or, if the bill is endorsed in blank, that they are the bearer in possession. This typically involves checking identification documents and comparing signatures where relevant.

However, the carrier's verification duty has limits. The carrier is not required to investigate the genuineness of signatures or the validity of transfers. If endorsements appear regular on their face and the presenter has proper identification, the carrier can deliver. Questions about whether endorsements were forged or transfers were invalid are matters between the parties to those transactions, not the carrier's responsibility.

Australian courts recognise these limitations.

---

[28] [1959] AC 576

In *Motis Exports Ltd v Dampskibsselskabet AF 1912* [29] followed in Australia, the court acknowledged that carriers cannot be expected to investigate complex questions of ownership. The carrier's duty is to check that the documentary chain appears regular and that the presenter appears to be entitled based on the documents.

8.2.3 Delivery Location

The carrier's obligation is to deliver at the port or place specified in the bill of lading. For traditional port-to-port bills, this means at the discharge port. The carrier must make goods available to the bill holder at that location, typically at the carrier's terminal or berth.

The *Hague-Visby Rules*, as implemented in Schedule 1A to the *Carriage of Goods by Sea Act 1991 (Cth)*, define the carrier's period of responsibility as running from loading to discharge. Article I(e) defines "carriage of goods" as covering "the period from the time when the goods are loaded on to the time when they are discharged from the ship." This suggests the carrier's delivery obligation is satisfied when goods are discharged from the vessel.

However, many modern bills extend the carrier's responsibility beyond vessel discharge. Multimodal and door-to-door bills may require delivery to inland destinations. Container bills often include terms about delivery from container terminals. The carrier must deliver at the location specified in the bill, which may be beyond the port.

Problems arise when the carrier cannot deliver at the specified location due to circumstances beyond its control - port congestion, strikes, berth unavailability, war, or natural disasters.

Most bills contain "liberty clauses" permitting delivery at alternative locations in specified circumstances. Courts generally uphold such clauses if they are clear and the carrier acts reasonably, but delivery at unauthorised alternative locations without contractual permission may constitute breach.

8.2.4 Timing of Delivery

---

[29] [2000] 1 Lloyd's Rep 211

Bills of lading typically do not specify exact delivery dates but rather provide that goods will be carried to the destination with reasonable dispatch. The carrier must make goods available for delivery within a reasonable time after the vessel arrives at the discharge port.

What constitutes "reasonable time" depends on circumstances. For break-bulk cargo, discharge may take days or weeks depending on cargo volume and port operations. For containerised cargo, discharge is typically quicker - containers may be unloaded within hours or days. After discharge, the carrier must make goods available at the terminal or designated delivery point.

The *Hague-Visby Rules* do not expressly address delivery timing, though delay in delivery may constitute a breach of the carrier's obligation to proceed with reasonable dispatch. Some jurisdictions have developed "reasonable time" standards through case law, considering factors like the nature of goods, port practices, and any special circumstances.

If goods are not claimed promptly after being made available, the carrier may be entitled to place them in warehouse storage and claim storage charges. Most bills contain terms addressing unclaimed cargo, permitting the carrier to warehouse goods at the cargo owner's expense after notice.

8.2.5 Delivery of Part Cargo

Sometimes only part of a consignment can be delivered, raising questions about whether the carrier can deliver part against surrender of the bill. Generally, the bill represents the entire consignment, and the carrier should not deliver part while retaining part.

If partial delivery occurs, several approaches are possible:

- The carrier might endorse the bill noting partial delivery and return it to the holder for claiming the remainder.
- The carrier might retain the bill and issue a delivery order for the remainder.
- The parties might agree to split delivery with appropriate documentation.

These solutions are imperfect. Endorsing the bill to note partial delivery may affect its negotiability. Retaining the bill deprives the holder of the document needed to deal with the remainder. The better practice is to avoid partial delivery situations by issuing separate bills for separable portions of cargo at the time of shipment.

8.3 Consequences of Misdelivery

8.3.1 Strict Liability for Delivery Without Bills

Delivering goods without requiring presentation of the bill of lading constitutes misdelivery for which the carrier is strictly liable. The carrier cannot defend by showing that delivery was made to the actual owner or that the person receiving delivery was in fact entitled. The right to delivery flows from the bill, not from ownership.

This principle was firmly established in *Sze Hai Tong Bank Ltd v Rambler Cycle Co Ltd*[30], a Privy Council decision followed in Australia. The carrier delivered bicycles to the consignee without production of the bill of lading. The bank held the bill as security for advances. Despite the fact that the consignee was the actual buyer and owner of the bicycles, the Privy Council held the carrier liable to the bank for delivering without the bill.

Lord Denning explained:

"The contract is to deliver to the person entitled under the bill of lading in exchange for the bill of lading...The duty of the shipowner is to deliver the goods to the person who, under the terms of the contract of carriage, is entitled to delivery and that is the person entitled under the bill of lading."

Australian courts have consistently applied this strict approach.

In *Kupang Setia Sdn Bhd v Bali Shipping Pte Ltd* (2001), an unreported New South Wales Supreme Court decision, the carrier delivered containerised cargo without bills. The court held this was a fundamental breach regardless of whether the receiver was entitled to the goods.

8.3.2 Loss of Right to Limit Liability

---

[30] [1959] AC 576

The consequences of misdelivery extend beyond liability for the value of the goods. Carriers who deliberately deliver without bills may lose the right to limit liability under the Hague-Visby Rules and other contractual limitation provisions.

In *Motis Exports Ltd v Dampskibsselskabet AF 1912* [31], the English Court of Appeal (in a decision followed in Australia) held that deliberate delivery without production of bills of lading constituted a breach going to the root of the contract. The carrier could not rely on the package limitation in the *Hague-Visby Rules* because the deliberate breach was fundamentally inconsistent with the contract.

Longmore LJ stated:

"If a shipowner does not insist on production of the bill of lading at the port of discharge, he is not performing his obligation under the contract of carriage...Deliberate delivery of goods without presentation of the bill of lading is conduct which is so inconsistent with the contract that it must be taken to be a repudiation of it."

The Australian position follows this approach. *Article IV rule 5 of the Hague-Visby Rules*, as implemented in *Schedule 1A to the Carriage of Goods by Sea Act 1991 (Cth)*, provides limitation of liability for loss or damage to goods. However, courts have held that fundamental breaches like deliberate misdelivery fall outside the scope of the Rules' protection.

This means carriers face potential liability for the full value of the cargo, not merely the per-package or per-kilo limitation. For high-value cargo, this exposure can be substantial - millions of dollars rather than the modest amounts allowed under limitation provisions.

8.3.3 Measure of Damages

When carriers misdeliver, the measure of damages is typically the value of the goods at the time and place where delivery should have occurred. This compensates the lawful bill holder for being deprived of the goods.

---

[31] [2000] 1 Lloyd's Rep 211

If goods have been delivered to the wrong person, that person becomes liable for conversion (wrongful dealing with goods) to the rightful owner. The carrier's liability to the bill holder exists concurrently with the recipient's liability. The bill holder might choose to sue either or both, though can only recover once.

In assessing damages, courts consider:

- The market value of goods at the intended delivery location
- Any special value to the particular cargo owner (subject to remoteness principles)
- Currency conversion if goods were to be sold in foreign markets.
- Loss of profit if goods were intended for resale.
- Any mitigation achieved (such as recovery from the wrongful recipient)

Interest typically runs from the date of misdelivery to judgment. Courts may also award costs on an indemnity basis where carriers have acted with deliberate disregard for their obligations.

8.3.4 Claims by Multiple Parties

Misdelivery situations sometimes involve competing claims by multiple parties. The shipper might claim, the endorsee of the bill might claim, and the person who actually received delivery might assert ownership. How are these claims resolved?

The general principle is that the lawful holder of the bill at the time of misdelivery has the primary claim against the carrier. That person was entitled to delivery and was wrongfully deprived of it. Other parties claiming interest in the goods must resolve their disputes among themselves. The carrier faces liability to the bill holder regardless of who ultimately proves to own the goods.

However, if the carrier delivers in good faith to someone reasonably appearing to be entitled, and later a bill holder emerges claiming the goods, the carrier may face difficult choices. The carrier cannot obtain the goods back from the person to whom they were delivered (who may have consumed or sold them). The carrier must compensate the bill holder for the loss.

This demonstrates why the bill of lading system requires strict adherence. The carrier who delivers against the bill is protected, and even if it later emerges that someone else actually owned the goods, the carrier's obligation was to the bill holder. But the carrier who delivers without the bill faces liability to bill holders regardless of actual ownership.

8.4 Letters of Indemnity and Delivery Without Bills

8.4.1 The Commercial Practice

Despite clear legal principles requiring delivery against bills, commercial practice often involves delivery without bills against letters of indemnity (LOIs). When vessels arrive before bills of lading reach the destination, cargo sits at expensive terminals incurring demurrage. Consignees demand immediate release. Carriers face commercial pressure to deliver despite lack of bills.

The compromise is that consignees provide LOI's as contractual undertakings to indemnify the carrier against any claims arising from delivering without the bill. The LOI typically states that the indemnifier will compensate the carrier for any loss if someone later presents the bill and claims the goods. Often the LOI is counter-guaranteed by a bank, providing financial backing.

A typical LOI includes:

- Identification of the shipment and bill of lading number
- Request for delivery without production of the bill
- Undertaking to produce the bill when received
- Indemnity for all consequences of delivering without the bill.
- Agreement to pay all costs and expenses of defending claims.
- Submission to jurisdiction
- Often a bank counter-guarantee

This practice is widespread, particularly in containerised liner trades and short sea routes. Some estimate that a significant percentage of container deliveries occur against LOIs rather than bills. The practice reflects the practical reality that modern ships move faster than paper documents.

8.4.2 Legal Effect of LOIs

Despite their commercial prevalence, LOIs do not legitimise delivery without bills. The carrier who delivers against an LOI still commits misdelivery and remains liable to the lawful bill holder. The LOI creates a contractual right for the carrier to claim indemnity from the LOI provider, but does not eliminate the carrier's breach of the carriage contract.

This was established in Sze Hai Tong Bank v Rambler Cycle [32]. The carrier delivered against an LOI. When the bank (holding the bill as security) sued, the carrier could not defeat the claim by pointing to the LOI. The carrier remained liable to the bank; the LOI merely gave the carrier a claim against the indemnifier.

Lord Denning explained:

"The letter of indemnity is of no avail as a defence. It does not alter the contract between the bank and the shipowners. It remains the duty of the shipowners to deliver the goods to the person entitled under the bill of lading. If they fail to do so, they are liable in damages."

The position in Australia follows this principle. LOIs provide commercial arrangements for risk allocation between carriers and consignees, but do not affect the carrier's legal liability for misdelivery to lawful bill holders.

8.4.3 Enforceability of LOIs

If LOIs do not prevent carrier liability for misdelivery, can carriers at least recover under the LOI from the indemnifier? The answer is: sometimes, but not always. The enforceability of LOIs is limited by considerations of public policy and illegality.

Where delivery without the bill involves fraud, such as when the carrier knows the consignee is not entitled to the goods, or when the LOI provider is deliberately defrauding the bill holder, courts refuse to enforce the LOI as contrary to public policy. An agreement to indemnify for fraudulent conduct is unenforceable.

In Brown Jenkinson & Co Ltd v Percy Dalton (London) Ltd [33], followed in Australia, the court held that a letter of indemnity given to induce a carrier to issue a false bill of lading could not be enforced. The agreement was based on an illegal act (issuing a false document) and was therefore void.

---

[32] [1959] AC 576
[33] [1957] 2 QB 621

Similarly, if an LOI is given to induce delivery without bills when the indemnifier knows this will defraud the bill holder, the LOI may be unenforceable. However, if the LOI is given in good faith circumstances, such as where documents are genuinely delayed and the indemnifier reasonably believes they are entitled to the goods, courts are more likely to enforce it.

Australian courts apply these principles cautiously.

In Lakeport Navigation Co Panama SA v Waipawa Shipping Ltd [34], the New South Wales Court of Appeal considered an LOI in a shipping dispute. While the particular case involved different issues, the court confirmed that LOIs could be unenforceable where they involved illegal conduct or fraud.

8.4.4 Bank Counter-Guarantees

To strengthen LOIs, consignees often arrange for banks to provide counter-guarantees. The bank undertakes to pay the carrier if the LOI indemnifier defaults. This gives carriers financial security, particularly where indemnifiers might be unable to pay if substantial claims arise.

Bank counter-guarantees are generally enforceable unless the underlying LOI is void for illegality or fraud. If the carrier legitimately claims under the LOI based on a bill holder's claim, the bank must pay under its counter-guarantee. Banks typically pay first and pursue reimbursement from their customer (the indemnifier) later.

However, banks can refuse payment if the carrier's claim involves fraud or if the delivery without bills was done dishonestly. The counter-guarantee does not require banks to fund fraudulent operations. If a court finds the LOI unenforceable due to illegality, the counter-guarantee falls with it.

8.4.5 Risk Assessment for Carriers

Carriers accepting LOIs must assess the risks:

Low risk situations: Where documents are genuinely delayed, the consignee appears clearly entitled, and a reputable bank provides the counter-

[34] (1992) 27 NSWLR 56

guarantee, the risk may be acceptable. The carrier faces some legal risk but has practical recourse if problems arise.

High risk situations: Where the consignee's entitlement is unclear, no bank counter-guarantee exists, the consignee is unknown or financially weak, or there are signs of fraud, carriers should refuse to deliver without bills. The legal and financial risks are too great.

Prudent carriers establish policies for LOI acceptance, including:

- Requirements for bank counter-guarantees above certain value thresholds
- Know-your-customer checks on indemnifiers.
- Verification that bills were actually issued and documents genuinely delayed.
- Refusal where fraud indicators exist.
- Time limits on how long after vessel arrival delivery without bills is permitted.

Even with safeguards, carriers accepting LOIs assume significant risk. The safest course is always to require bills, but commercial pressures make this impractical in many trades.

8.5 Special Delivery Situations

8.5.1 Delivery When Bills Are Lost

Bills of lading are sometimes lost in transit, lost by couriers, misplaced by cargo owners, or destroyed in disasters. When bills are lost, the lawful owner cannot present them to claim delivery, but the carrier cannot deliver without presentation. This creates a dilemma.

The solution requires the cargo owner to establish entitlement through other evidence and provide security for the carrier's protection. The cargo owner might:

- Provide evidence of ownership and loss (shipping documents, correspondence, shipping instructions)
- Obtain a court order requiring the carrier to deliver.

- Provide an LOI with bank counter-guarantee indemnifying the carrier against claims by anyone presenting the original bill.

Courts have jurisdiction to order delivery despite lost bills where sufficient evidence of entitlement and loss exists. The court may require the cargo owner to provide security or undertakings protecting the carrier. This balances the cargo owner's right to goods against the carrier's need for protection if the lost bill resurfaces.

Carriers face difficult decisions with lost bills. If they deliver based on insufficient evidence and someone later presents the original bill, the carrier is liable for misdelivery. If they refuse to deliver despite legitimate claims and adequate security, they may be liable for unreasonable refusal. Careful assessment and legal advice are essential.

8.5.2 Delivery to Straight Bills (Non-Negotiable Bills)

Straight bills of lading (non-negotiable bills naming a specific consignee) present different delivery issues. As discussed in Chapter 3, straight bills are generally not full documents of title because they are not transferable. The named consignee is entitled to delivery by virtue of being named, not by possessing the bill.

Should carriers require presentation of straight bills before delivery?

Opinions differ. Some argue that even straight bills should be surrendered as evidence that the person claiming delivery is indeed the named consignee. Others argue that straight bills need not be presented - the carrier verifies the claimant's identity and delivers if they are the named consignee.

Section 11 of the *Carriage of Goods by Sea Act 1991 (Cth)* applies to non-negotiable bills as well as negotiable ones, transferring rights of suit to consignees. However, the section does not explicitly require surrender of straight bills for delivery.

In practice, many carriers require surrender of straight bills as a matter of prudence, even though legal requirements may be less stringent than for order bills. This provides evidence that delivery was made to the right person and prevents disputes. However, if straight bills are delayed and the consignee provides satisfactory identification, carriers may deliver without the bill with less risk than would apply to order bills.

8.5.3 Delivery of Goods Shipped on Deck

Goods shipped on deck require special consideration. Article I(c) of the Hague-Visby Rules provides that "goods" includes goods carried on deck only if such carriage is in accordance with agreement or custom of the trade. Unauthorised deck carriage may affect the carrier's rights and obligations.

When delivering deck cargo, carriers should verify that:

- The bill authorises deck carriage or it is customary in the trade.
- The cargo actually was carried on deck (if unauthorised deck carriage, this may constitute deviation affecting rights)
- The cargo remains in apparent good condition despite deck exposure.

For containerised cargo, deck carriage is now standard practice, and most container bills contain clauses authorising it. Carriers routinely deliver containers that were carried on deck without special procedures. However, if deck carriage was unauthorised and cargo was damaged, delivery may trigger claims for the damage caused by unauthorised deck carriage.

8.5.4 Delivery of Damaged or Deteriorated Goods

When goods arrive damaged or deteriorated, delivery presents challenges. The carrier must deliver what remains, but both carrier and cargo owner should document the condition to preserve evidence for potential claims.

Good practice includes:

- Joint inspection by carrier and cargo owner (or their representatives) of damaged goods
- Detailed notation of damage on delivery receipts or terminal documents
- Photography of damage before delivery
- Retention of packaging or samples if appropriate
- Immediate notice to surveyors and insurers

The carrier should not refuse to deliver merely because goods are damaged. The carrier's obligation is to deliver such goods as remain, and the cargo owner has the right to receive them even if damaged. Refusal to deliver damaged goods may itself constitute breach.

However, if goods have deteriorated to the point of being dangerous (such as rotted foodstuffs or damaged chemical containers), carriers may have the right or even the duty to refuse delivery until the cargo owner arranges safe disposal. Most bills contain terms addressing disposal of goods that have become dangerous or valueless.

8.5.5 Delivery of Partial Shipments and Short Delivery

Short delivery - delivery of less than the quantity stated in the bill is one of the most common cargo disputes. When the carrier delivers less than the bill specifies, the cargo owner may claim for the shortage.

At delivery, carriers should:

- Count or weigh goods being delivered and compare to bill of lading statements.
- Note any shortages on delivery documentation.
- Require cargo owner signature acknowledging the quantity delivered.
- Investigate causes of shortage (theft, misdirection, counting error at loading)
- Preserve evidence regarding quantity shipped and delivered.

If the bill contained "shipper's load and count" qualifications, these may protect the carrier from shortage claims, as discussed in Chapter 5. However, even qualified bills create liability for shortages that the carrier should have detected or that occurred through the carrier's negligence.

When shortages are discovered at delivery, the cargo owner should give immediate written notice to the carrier as required by Article III rule 6 of the Hague-Visby Rules. Failure to give timely notice may bar claims or create evidential difficulties.

8.6 Port Procedures and Practical Delivery

8.6.1 Container Terminal Operations

Modern containerised cargo delivery occurs primarily at container terminals rather than alongside vessels. The vessel discharges containers to the terminal, and cargo owners or their agents collect containers from the terminal. This creates issues about when and where the carrier's responsibility ends.

Typical container delivery procedures involve:

- Vessel discharges containers to terminal
- Terminal stores containers in container yard
- Carrier (or its agent) notifies cargo owner that goods are available.
- Cargo owner presents bill of lading (or LOI) to carrier's office.
- Carrier issues delivery order or electronic release to terminal
- Cargo owner presents delivery order and identification to terminal.
- Terminal releases container to cargo owner's truck

At what point has "delivery" occurred for legal purposes?

The *Hague-Visby Rules* apply only until goods are discharged from the vessel. After discharge, liability is governed by the bill of lading terms and general law. Most container bills extend carrier responsibility to include delivery from the terminal but specify that liability ceases once containers are released to the cargo owner or their agent.

8.6.2 Delivery Orders and Release Documentation

After accepting presentation of bills of lading, carriers issue delivery orders to terminals authorising release of cargo. Delivery orders are internal documents from carrier to terminal, not documents of title. The cargo owner's right to delivery derives from the bill of lading; the delivery order is merely the carrier's instruction to the terminal to release goods to that person.

Modern practice increasingly uses electronic release systems. When the cargo owner presents the bill (or LOI) at the carrier's office, the carrier electronically notifies the terminal to release cargo to that party. The cargo owner may receive a PIN code or electronic authorisation that they present at the terminal gate.

These electronic systems streamline delivery but create some legal uncertainty. If a terminal releases cargo based on an electronic instruction that proves to be unauthorised (due to system hacking or internal fraud), who bears responsibility? The carrier remains ultimately liable for misdelivery, but may have recourse against the terminal if the terminal failed to follow proper procedures.

8.6.3 Documentation and Proof of Delivery

Carriers should obtain and retain proof of delivery, including:

- Signed delivery receipts or terminal gate receipts showing who collected goods.
- Bill of lading retained with appropriate surrender notation.
- Delivery order copies
- Electronic records of release authorisations
- Identification documents of the person collecting goods.
- Any notations about damage or shortage

This documentation is essential if delivery disputes later arise. The carrier must prove it delivered to the rightful person. Clear records showing proper presentation of bills, verification of identity, and release of goods provide this proof.

The cargo owner also benefits from proper documentation. Signed receipts acknowledge the quantity and apparent condition of goods received, which is relevant to subsequent claims for shortage or damage.

8.7 Refusal to Deliver and Carrier's Lien

8.7.1 The Carrier's Lien for Freight and Charges

Carriers have a possessory lien over cargo for unpaid freight, demurrage, and other charges arising from the carriage. This lien entitles the carrier to retain possession of goods until charges are paid. The lien is recognised both at common law and through express terms in bills of lading.

The carrier's lien exists for:

- Freight (if not prepaid)

- Demurrage and detention charges
- Costs of storage or special handling
- General average contributions
- Other charges specifically provided for in the bill.

The lien does not extend to unrelated charges. If a carrier is owed money by the cargo owner for previous shipments, the carrier cannot hold current cargo as leverage. The lien attaches only to charges related to the particular shipment evidenced by that bill.

To exercise the lien, the carrier simply refuses delivery until charges are paid. The cargo owner must pay to obtain delivery. If the cargo owner refuses or cannot pay, the carrier may be entitled (depending on bill of lading terms and applicable law) to sell the goods and recover charges from the proceeds.

8.7.2 Conflicts Between Lien Rights and Delivery Obligations

Tension can arise between the carrier's lien and the carrier's delivery obligation. The bill holder presents the bill demanding delivery, but freight is unpaid. Can the carrier refuse delivery?

The answer depends on whether freight is "prepaid" or "collect." If the bill states "freight prepaid," the carrier has acknowledged that freight is paid and cannot refuse delivery for non-payment of freight (though may refuse for other unpaid charges like demurrage). If the bill states "freight collect," the carrier can refuse delivery until freight is paid.

Problems arise when bills incorrectly state freight status. If a bill states "prepaid" but freight was not actually paid, the carrier is generally estopped from claiming freight from the bill holder, and the carrier's remedy is against the shipper. The carrier must deliver despite non-payment by the shipper.

This protection of bill holders reflects the document of title function. A transferee taking a bill stating "freight prepaid" should be able to rely on that statement without investigating whether the shipper actually paid. The carrier's statements in the bill bind the carrier against third parties.

8.7.3 Sale of Goods Under Lien

If cargo remains unclaimed and charges unpaid, carriers may eventually sell goods to recover charges. However, this power is not unlimited. Most bills of lading contain terms specifying:

- When sale is permitted (after what period of non-payment/non-collection)
- Notice requirements before sale
- Method of sale (public auction, private sale, etc.)
- Application of proceeds (to charges, with balance to cargo owner)

Even with contractual terms, carriers must act reasonably. Sale at undervalue may make the carrier liable for the difference. Sale without adequate notice may be actionable. Carriers exercising lien rights should follow contractual procedures carefully and document their actions.

Australian state legislation also addresses carriers' liens and sale rights. The *Mercantile Law Act 1936 (SA)* and equivalent legislation in other states contain provisions governing the sale of uncollected goods by bailees, including carriers. These provisions may apply in addition to contractual terms.

8.7.4 Delivery Against Bank Guarantees

When freight or other charges are disputed, cargo owners sometimes offer bank guarantees or bonds in lieu of payment. The carrier releases cargo against the guarantee, which secures payment if charges are ultimately determined to be owing.

Bank guarantees provide carriers with financial security while avoiding delay in cargo release. If dispute resolution determines charges are owing, the carrier can call on the guarantee. If charges are not owing, the guarantee lapses. This balances the carrier's need for security against the cargo owner's need for prompt delivery.

Carriers should ensure bank guarantees:

- Cover the full amount potentially owing (charges plus interest and costs)
- Are from reputable financial institutions.
- Are unconditional or subject only to reasonable conditions.
- Have adequate duration (until disputes can be resolved)
- Specify the governing law and jurisdiction.

8.8 Delivery in Specific Contexts

8.8.1 Delivery in Documentary Credit Transactions

Documentary credit transactions involve complex delivery considerations because banks hold bills as security. The typical sequence is:

1. Seller ships goods and obtains bill of lading
2. Seller presents bill to advising/confirming bank
3. Bank pays seller and takes bill as security
4. Bank forwards bill to issuing bank
5. Issuing bank forwards bill to buyer/applicant
6. Buyer pays bank and receives bill
7. Buyer presents bill to carrier and obtains delivery

If the buyer defaults in payment to the issuing bank, the bank retains the bill and may itself claim delivery to sell the goods. The carrier must honour the bank's presentation of the bill, even though the bank is not the buyer of the goods.

Problems arise if carriers release cargo before bills arrive at destination banks. The bank may have paid the seller relying on the bill as security, only to find goods have been delivered without bills. The carrier's misdelivery makes the carrier liable to the bank for the full value of the cargo.

8.8.2 Delivery Where Bills Have Been Pledged

Bills of lading are commonly pledged as security for loans. A cargo owner needing financing may pledge bills to a bank, which holds them as collateral. If the cargo owner defaults, the bank may present the bill to claim delivery and sell the goods.

Carriers should verify the pledgee's authority when banks present bills. Typically the pledge is evidenced by:

- Endorsement of the bill to the bank or to the bank's order
- Accompanying loan documentation (which the carrier need not see but confirms existence)
- The bank's possession of the bill

Once satisfied that the bank holds the bill as pledgee, the carrier must deliver to the bank or to the bank's designee. The carrier cannot refuse delivery merely because the original shipper or buyer objects. The bill is the document of title, and the bank holding it is entitled to delivery.

8.8.3 Delivery in Insolvency Situations

Insolvency of shippers, consignees, or cargo owners complicates delivery. If the bill holder becomes bankrupt or insolvent, questions arise about who is entitled to delivery - the liquidator, administrator, secured creditors, or someone else?

Generally, the carrier must deliver to whoever presents the bill as lawful holder. If the liquidator or administrator obtains the bill (as representing the insolvent estate), the carrier delivers to them. If a secured creditor holds the bill as security, the carrier delivers to them.

Difficulties arise if the carrier knows of insolvency, but no one presents the bill or claims delivery. The carrier should not deliver to the insolvent entity without the bill merely because they were the named consignee. The carrier should await presentation by whoever holds the bill - likely the liquidator or a secured creditor.

Australian insolvency law provides some guidance. *The Corporations Act 2001 (Cth)* addresses rights of receivers, liquidators, and administrators. These officers have powers to collect assets of the insolvent entity, including goods in transit evidenced by bills of lading. They may demand transfer of bills from the insolvent entity and then present those bills to carriers for delivery.

8.9 Concurrent and Conflicting Claims to Delivery

8.9.1 Multiple Bill Holders

Where bills are issued in sets of multiple originals, problems arise if different originals come into different hands. Each original is theoretically sufficient for delivery, but the carrier should deliver only once, to the first presenter.

Bills typically contain clauses stating "one of which being accomplished, the others to stand void." This means delivery against one original discharges the carrier's obligation. However, if the carrier delivers to the first presenter without investigating whether other originals exist in other hands, and those other holders later claim, the carrier may face liability.

Best practice is to require presentation of all originals in the set, or at least to verify that the presenter has all originals or has a reasonable explanation for their absence. If different originals are held by different parties due to fraud or irregular transfers, the carrier faces difficult choices and should seek legal advice before delivering.

8.9.2 Conflicting Claims Between Holder and Actual Owner

Sometimes the lawful bill holder is not the actual owner of the goods. This can occur through fraud, disputes over sale contracts, or documentary irregularities. If both the bill holder and someone claiming to be the actual owner demand delivery, whom should the carrier deliver to?

The answer is clear: the carrier must deliver to the bill holder. The bill of lading is the document of title, and the carrier's obligation is to the person presenting the bill. Disputes about who actually owns the goods are for the claimants to resolve among themselves, and are not the carrier's concern.

If the carrier knows of disputes about ownership, the carrier should not be drawn into them. The carrier delivers to the bill holder. If the actual owner believes the bill was obtained by fraud, the owner must pursue remedies against the fraudster; suing the carrier for delivering to the bill holder is not available.

This rule protects carriers from being caught in disputes between cargo interests. It also maintains the integrity of the bill of lading system. If carriers could refuse delivery to bill holders based on third-party claims of ownership, bills would lose their character as documents of title.

8.9.3 Competing Claims by Bill Holder and Government Authorities

Government authorities may claim goods for various reasons - customs violations, import restrictions, seizure for debts or penalties, or requisitioning. When authorities demand cargo, can the carrier deliver despite bill holders' claims?

Generally, carriers must comply with lawful government seizures. If customs properly seizes goods for smuggling or import violations, the carrier cannot refuse and must surrender the goods to authorities. The bill holder's claim is against the government or the party responsible for the violation, not the carrier.

However, the carrier should verify that government claims are lawful and properly documented. Mere assertions by officials without proper paperwork should not prompt delivery. The carrier is entitled to see seizure orders, court orders, or proper documentation justifying government taking of cargo.

If the carrier delivers to government authorities based on apparently valid legal process, and it later emerges the process was defective, the carrier may still be protected if it acted reasonably. Courts recognise that carriers cannot be expected to litigate government claims. If legal process appears valid, compliance is reasonable.

8.10 Delivery of Dangerous Goods

8.10.1 Shipper's Obligations Regarding Dangerous Goods

Article IV rule 6 of the Hague-Visby Rules addresses dangerous goods. It provides that goods of an inflammable, explosive, or dangerous nature shipped without the carrier's knowledge and consent may be landed, destroyed, or rendered innocuous at any time without compensation. If shipper knew or ought to have known of the dangerous nature, the shipper is liable for damage.

This provision protects carriers from undeclared dangerous cargo. If the shipper fails to declare goods as dangerous, the carrier may refuse delivery or may dispose of them without liability. However, if the carrier knew of and consented to the dangerous nature, the carrier cannot later refuse delivery or dispose of goods without justification.

At delivery, if dangerous goods have become more dangerous (such as through deterioration or damage to packaging), the carrier may refuse delivery and require the shipper or cargo owner to arrange safe disposal. The carrier is not obliged to deliver goods that present safety hazards.

8.10.2 Carrier's Rights and Obligations

When dangerous goods arrive at destination, carriers must balance delivery obligations against safety concerns. If goods remain safe for delivery, the carrier should deliver normally against presentation of bills. If goods have become dangerous, the carrier may:

- Require the cargo owner to arrange appropriate disposal.
- If immediate danger exists, dispose of goods and claim costs from the shipper/cargo owner.
- Obtain government assistance if goods present public safety risks.

Most bills of lading contain detailed dangerous goods clauses expanding on the Hague-Visby Rules' basic provisions. These clauses typically:

- Define what constitutes "dangerous" goods broadly.
- Require shippers to declare dangerous nature and provide Material Safety Data Sheets
- Give carriers rights to refuse carriage, discharge, or dispose of dangerous goods.
- Make shippers liable for all consequences of shipping dangerous goods.
- Require compliance with IMDG Code (International Maritime Dangerous Goods Code) and other regulations.

8.11 Conclusion

The carrier's obligation to deliver goods against presentation of the bill of lading is fundamental to the entire system of bills as documents of title. This obligation must be strictly observed to maintain the integrity of international trade and the security that bills provide. Yet carriers face significant practical pressures to deliver without bills, particularly when vessels arrive before documents.

The Australian legal position is clear: carriers who deliver without bills commit misdelivery and face strict liability for the full value of goods. Letters of indemnity provide some practical protection but do not legitimise misdelivery and may not be enforceable in all circumstances. Carriers accepting LOIs assume substantial risks.

Understanding delivery obligations requires appreciating both the legal rules and the commercial realities. Carriers must balance legal compliance against commercial demands. Cargo owners must understand their rights and the documentation needed to claim delivery. Banks and traders must ensure their security interests are protected through proper handling of bills.

Modern developments - containerisation, electronic communications, and faster vessels have made traditional bill of lading delivery procedures increasingly difficult. Electronic bills of lading offer potential solutions by enabling instant transmission of documents. However, until electronic bills achieve widespread adoption, the tension between legal requirements and practical necessity will continue.

The principles examined in this chapter - strict delivery obligations, the consequences of misdelivery, the limited protection of LOIs, and special situations requiring careful handling, and provide the framework for navigating delivery in practice. Subsequent chapters will examine the limitations and exceptions that protect carriers (Chapter 9) and contemporary challenges facing bills of lading (Chapter 10). The delivery obligations explored here implement the document of title function, making bills of lading work as instruments facilitating international trade.

Chapter 9: Limitations and Exceptions in Bills of Lading

9.1 Introduction

While carriers have extensive obligations regarding the care and delivery of cargo, they are not insurers of the goods. The law recognises that maritime carriage involves inherent risks beyond the carrier's control - perils of the sea, acts of God, and various other hazards that may damage or destroy cargo despite the carrier's best efforts.

The *Hague-Visby Rules*, as implemented in Australian law through the *Carriage of Goods by Sea Act 1991 (Cth)*, establish a balanced regime of carrier liability, combining minimum obligations with defined exceptions and limitations.

This chapter examines these exceptions and limitations, their interpretation by Australian courts, and their practical application in cargo claims.

Understanding the limitations and exceptions framework is essential for all parties in maritime commerce. Carriers must know the scope of their protection and the circumstances where limitations do not apply. Cargo owners must understand what losses they can recover and what risks they bear. Insurers must assess their exposure based on gaps in carrier liability. The interplay between carrier obligations, exceptions, limitations, and insurance creates the risk allocation structure underpinning international trade.

9.2 The Framework of the Hague-Visby Rules

9.2.1 The Basic Liability Structure

The *Hague-Visby Rules* establish a three-tier framework for carrier liability:

Tier 1 - Carrier's Obligations (Article III rules 1-2): The carrier must exercise due diligence to make the vessel seaworthy and must properly care for cargo. These are the carrier's fundamental duties.

Tier 2 - Exceptions from Liability (Article IV rule 2): Even if the carrier has fulfilled its duties, the carrier is not liable for loss or damage arising from specified excepted perils - seventeen enumerated categories including perils of the sea, fire, and inherent vice.

Tier 3 - Limitation of Liability (Article IV rule 5): Even where the carrier is liable, the carrier can limit liability to specified amounts per package or per kilo unless the cargo owner declared higher value.

This structure means cargo claims follow a logical progression:

1. Did loss/damage occur while goods were in the carrier's care?
2. Did the carrier breach its obligations (fail due diligence or proper care)?
3. If yes, does an exception apply to relieve the carrier from liability?
4. If the carrier remains liable, can the carrier limit the amount of liability?

9.2.2 The Burden of Proof

Article IV rule 1 of the Hague-Visby Rules provides that none of the Article IV exceptions relieves the carrier from obligations under Article III to exercise due diligence regarding seaworthiness and to properly care for cargo. The carrier cannot invoke exceptions if the carrier's own breach caused or contributed to the loss.

The burden of proof operates as follows:

Cargo owner's initial burden: The cargo owner must prove that goods were shipped in good condition (established by a clean bill of lading) and were delivered damaged or not delivered at all. This establishes a prima facie case of carrier liability.

Carrier's burden regarding exceptions: Once the cargo owner establishes loss or damage, the burden shifts to the carrier to prove that loss falls within one of the Article IV rule 2 exceptions.

Cargo owner's rebuttal: If the carrier establishes an exception applies, the burden shifts back to the cargo owner to prove that the carrier's negligence or breach of duty caused or contributed to the loss.

This burden-shifting framework was established in <u>*Gosse Millerd Ltd v Canadian Government Merchant Marine*</u> Ltd [35] and has been consistently applied by Australian courts.

In <u>*Shipping Corporation of India Ltd v Gamlen Chemical Co (A/Asia) Pty Ltd*</u> [36] the High Court of Australia confirmed this approach, emphasising that carriers cannot rely on exceptions where their own fault contributed to loss.

9.2.3 The Relationship Between Obligations and Exceptions

The exceptions in Article IV rule 2 are not absolute defences. They apply only where the carrier has fulfilled the obligations in Article III. If the carrier fails to exercise due diligence to make the vessel seaworthy, or fails to properly care for cargo, the carrier cannot rely on exceptions even if an excepted peril was also involved.

This principle prevents carriers from escaping liability through combinations of breach and excepted peril. For example, if a vessel is unseaworthy due to defective refrigeration equipment, and cargo deteriorates due to inadequate refrigeration, the carrier cannot claim the exception for "insufficiency of packing" or "inherent vice." The carrier's breach of the seaworthiness obligation caused the loss, and exceptions do not apply.

Australian courts strictly enforce this principle. In *Gamlen Chemical*, the High Court held that where cargo was damaged by water ingress through inadequately sealed hatches, the carrier could not rely on the "perils of the sea" exception. The unseaworthiness (inadequate hatch seals) was the effective cause of the damage, not the sea itself.

9.3 The Article III Obligations

9.3.1 Seaworthiness: Due Diligence Requirement

Article III rule 1 provides:

---

[35] [1929] AC 223
[36] (1980) 147 CLR 142,

"The carrier shall be bound before and at the beginning of the voyage to exercise due diligence to:

(a) Make the vessel seaworthy;
(b) Properly man, equip and supply the ship;
(c) Make the holds, refrigerating and cool chambers, and all other parts of the ship in which goods are carried, fit and safe for their reception, carriage and preservation."

This obligation is to exercise "due diligence, not to guarantee seaworthiness. The carrier must take reasonable steps to ensure seaworthiness but is not strictly liable if defects exist despite reasonable efforts.

Seaworthiness encompasses:

- Physical seaworthiness: The vessel's hull, machinery, and equipment must be sound and fit for the voyage.
- Cargo worthiness: Holds and cargo spaces must be fit for the particular cargo.
- Manning: Adequate crew with appropriate skills
- Equipment and supplies: Necessary equipment and supplies for the voyage

The due diligence standard requires carriers to:

- Properly survey and inspect vessels.
- Make necessary repairs before sailing.
- Engage competent contractors for maintenance.
- Ensure adequate crew training and competence.
- Provide proper equipment for cargo handling.
- Follow industry standards and practices.

Australian courts have examined the due diligence requirement in numerous cases. In *Maxine Footwear Co Ltd v Canadian Government Merchant Marine Ltd* [37] followed in Australia, the Privy Council held that due diligence requires the carrier to take reasonable steps to discover and remedy defects, but does not require absolute perfection.

[37] [1959] AC 589

9.3.2 Proper Care of Cargo

Article III rule 2 provides: "Subject to the provisions of Article IV, the carrier shall properly and carefully load, handle, stow, carry, keep, care for, and discharge the goods carried."

This obligation is more demanding than the seaworthiness obligation. It is not merely to exercise due diligence but to "properly and carefully" perform cargo operations. However, it is still a fault-based standard requiring reasonable care, not absolute liability.

"Properly and carefully" requires:

- Loading: Care in handling cargo when loading to avoid damage
- Stowage: Appropriate placement in the vessel, considering cargo characteristics
- Securing: Adequate lashing and securing to prevent shifting
- Care during voyage: Protection from weather, temperature control where needed.
- Discharge: Care when unloading to avoid damage

The carrier is liable for negligence in any of these operations. If cargo is damaged due to improper stowage, rough handling, inadequate securing, or other failure to exercise proper care, the carrier is liable unless an exception applies.

In *Gamlen Chemical*, cargo drums were inadequately secured and shifted during the voyage, causing damage. The High Court held this breached the Article III rule 2 obligation to properly stow and secure cargo. The carrier could not rely on the "perils of the sea" exception because the carrier's own negligence caused the damage.

9.3.3 Temporal Scope: "Before and at the Beginning of the Voyage"

The Article III rule 1 seaworthiness obligation applies "before and at the beginning of the voyage." This means the vessel must be seaworthy when it departs. If unseaworthiness develops during the voyage (such as machinery breakdown), this does not breach Article III rule 1, though it may breach Article III rule 2 if the carrier fails to properly respond to the problem.

The voyage begins when the vessel departs the loading port with the particular cargo. For multi-port loading voyages, courts have held that each departure from a loading port begins a new "voyage" for cargo already loaded, but the carrier's obligation is primarily to ensure seaworthiness at the commencement of the entire voyage.

The temporal limitation means carriers are not liable for unseaworthiness developing during the voyage unless it results from lack of due diligence before departure or unless the carrier fails to properly respond under Article III rule 2.

9.3.4 Non-Delegable Duty

A critical feature of the seaworthiness obligation is that it is personal and non-delegable. The carrier cannot escape liability by proving it engaged competent contractors to survey and repair the vessel. If contractors negligently fail to detect or repair defects, the carrier is liable.

Article IV rule 2(a) provides an exception for "act, neglect, or default of the master, mariner, pilot, or the servants of the carrier in the navigation or in the management of the ship." However, this exception does not extend to failures in making the vessel seaworthy. Negligence in navigation or management is excused; negligence in achieving seaworthiness before departure is not.

This distinction was established in *Elder, Dempster & Co v Paterson, Sochonis & Co* [38] and confirmed in Australia. Carriers remain liable for their contractors' negligence in pre-voyage preparation, but not for crew negligence in operating the vessel during the voyage.

9.4 The Article IV Rule 2 Exceptions

9.4.1 Overview of the Seventeen Exceptions

Article IV rule 2 lists seventeen categories of excepted perils. The carrier is not liable for loss or damage arising from these causes, provided the carrier has fulfilled its Article III obligations. The exceptions are:

---

[38] [1924] AC 522

(a) Act, neglect, or default of the master, mariner, pilot, or servants in navigation or management of the ship
(b) Fire, unless caused by actual fault or privity of the carrier
(c) Perils, dangers and accidents of the sea or other navigable waters
(d) Act of God
(e) Act of war
(f) Act of public enemies
(g) Arrest or restraint of princes, rulers or people, or seizure under legal process
(h) Quarantine restrictions
(i) Act or omission of the shipper or owner of the goods
(j) Strikes or lockouts or stoppage or restraint of labour
(k) Riots and civil commotions
(l) Saving or attempting to save life or property at sea
(m) Wastage in bulk or weight or any other loss or damage arising from inherent defect, quality or vice of the goods
(n) Insufficiency of packing
(o) Insufficiency or inadequacy of marks
(p) Latent defects not discoverable by due diligence
(q) Any other cause arising without the actual fault or privity of the carrier

These exceptions cover a wide range of perils reflecting the hazards of maritime carriage. They balance carrier obligations against recognition that some losses occur despite proper care.

9.4.2 Navigation and Management Exception (Article IV rule 2(a))

The exception for "act, neglect, or default...in the navigation or in the management of the ship" protects carriers from crew negligence in operating the vessel. This exception recognises that despite employing competent crew and properly maintaining vessels, human error in navigation or ship management may occur.

Navigation includes:

- Steering and conning the vessel
- Setting course and speed
- Plotting position
- Collision avoidance
- Entering and leaving ports

Management of the ship includes:

- Operating machinery
- Managing ballast
- Opening and closing hatches for ship operations
- Firefighting
- Damage control

The exception does NOT cover cargo operations. Negligence in loading, stowing, securing, or discharging cargo falls under Article III rule 2 obligations, not the navigation/management exception.

Distinguishing between management of ship and care of cargo is often difficult. In *Gosse Millerd Ltd v Canadian Government Merchant Marine Ltd* [39] the vessel's crew negligently admitted seawater while operating pumps. The House of Lords held this was "management of the ship" covered by the exception, even though it damaged cargo.

Australian courts have grappled with this distinction. The key question is whether the act primarily related to operating the vessel or to caring for cargo. Opening hatches to ventilate holds is ship management; opening hatches to inspect cargo is cargo care.

9.4.3 Fire Exception (Article IV rule 2(b))

The fire exception provides that carriers are not liable for damage by fire "unless caused by the actual fault or privity of the carrier." This is broader than other exceptions because it protects carriers from fire damage caused by crew negligence, which would not be protected under the navigation/management exception.

The exception applies to fires from any cause - electrical faults, spontaneous combustion, negligent smoking by crew, machinery overheating, etc, unless the carrier itself (the company, not crew) was at fault.

"Actual fault or privity of the carrier" means fault of the carrier company - directors, senior management, or the owner personally if an individual. Crew

---

[39] [1929] AC 223,

negligence is not "actual fault of the carrier" for this purpose. The carrier must have personally participated in or authorised the fault.

This exception is historically based on the difficulty of proving fire causes at sea and the recognition that fires can occur despite proper care. Modern firefighting equipment and investigation techniques have reduced the rationale, but the exception remains.

In *Lennard's Carrying Co Ltd v Asiatic Petroleum Co Ltd* [40], followed in Australia, the House of Lords held that "actual fault or privity" requires personal involvement of those who are the "directing mind and will" of the carrier company.

9.4.4 Perils of the Sea (Article IV rule 2(c))

"Perils of the sea" refers to fortuitous accidents or casualties of the sea; extraordinary action of wind and waves that could not reasonably be anticipated and guarded against. It does not cover ordinary wear and tear of the voyage or expected conditions.

Examples of perils of the sea include:

- Extraordinary storms and heavy weather
- Striking submerged objects (rocks, wrecks)
- Unexpected heavy seas causing cargo damage.
- Ingress of seawater through fortuitous circumstances

NOT perils of the sea:

- Ordinary weather for the route and season
- Seawater ingress due to poor hatch maintenance (this is unseaworthiness)
- Expected conditions that proper care would prevent.

The distinction is between expected maritime conditions (against which carriers must protect) and extraordinary or fortuitous events. In *Canada Rice Mills Ltd v Union Marine & General Insurance Co Ltd* [41], the Privy Council

---

[40] [1915] AC 705
[41] [1941] AC 55

stated that perils of the sea means *"fortuitous accidents or casualties of the seas"* distinct from ordinary action of wind and waves.

Australian courts apply this strict interpretation. In *Gamlen Chemical,* seawater damage through inadequate hatch seals was not a peril of the sea because it resulted from unseaworthiness, not fortuitous accident.

9.4.5 Act of God (Article IV rule 2(d))

"Act of God" refers to natural events of extraordinary and irresistible character - events that no human foresight can provide against and no human effort can resist. The standard is very high.

Examples might include:

- Extraordinary and unprecedented weather phenomena
- Earthquakes and tsunamis
- Lightning strikes causing direct damage.
- Volcanic eruptions affecting navigation.

The act must be truly extraordinary. Severe storms, while dangerous, are generally not "acts of God" if they are within the range of conditions that can be expected and guarded against. The carrier must prove the event was unforeseeable and irresistible despite all reasonable precautions.

This exception has limited application because most natural events affecting shipping, even if severe, can be anticipated and measures taken. The exception requires proof that no amount of care could have prevented the loss.

9.4.6 Inherent Vice (Article IV rule 2(m))

The inherent vice exception covers "wastage in bulk or weight or any other loss or damage arising from inherent defect, quality or vice of the goods." This recognises that some goods deteriorate through their own nature despite proper care.

Inherent vice means a characteristic of the goods themselves that causes deterioration without external influence. Examples include:

- Ripening of fruit
- Fermentation of organic materials
- Oxidation of metals
- Evaporation of volatile substances
- Spontaneous combustion of certain materials
- Natural deterioration of perishables

The carrier is not liable for damage from inherent vice because no amount of care can prevent it, and the goods' own nature causes the problem. However, the carrier remains liable if proper care could have prevented or minimised the damage.

For example, if refrigerated goods deteriorate because refrigeration equipment fails, this is not inherent vice - it is the carrier's failure to properly care for cargo. But if fruit ripens and deteriorates during carriage despite proper temperature control, this is inherent vice.

In *Albacora SRL v Westcott & Laurance Line Ltd* [42], followed in Australia, fish meal shipped in bulk overheated and damaged due to its propensity to generate heat. The court held this was inherent vice - the goods' own characteristics caused the damage despite reasonable care.

9.4.7 Insufficiency of Packing (Article IV rule 2(n))

The packing exception provides that carriers are not liable for loss or damage arising from "insufficiency of packing." This places the risk of inadequate packaging on the shipper who packed the goods.

To establish this exception, the carrier must prove:

- Packing was in fact insufficient for the voyage.
- The insufficiency caused the damage.
- Proper packing would have prevented the damage.
- The carrier exercised reasonable care in handling.

"Insufficiency of packing" includes:

- Inadequate protection against expected voyage conditions

---

[42] [1966] 2 Lloyd's Rep 53

- Inappropriate packaging materials
- Insufficient padding or cushioning
- Weak containers that break under normal handling
- Packaging that does not protect against moisture, temperature, or other foreseeable hazards.

The exception does NOT apply if:

- The carrier handled cargo roughly despite inadequate packing
- The carrier knew packaging was insufficient and should have rejected cargo or required re-packing
- Packaging would have been adequate but for the carrier's negligence

Australian courts require carriers to prove that packing insufficiency, not carrier negligence, caused the damage. In cases involving both inadequate packing and rough handling, courts may apportion responsibility.

9.4.8 Shipper's Act or Omission (Article IV rule 2(i))

The exception for "act or omission of the shipper or owner of the goods" covers damage caused by the shipper's fault. Examples include:

- Misdeclaration of goods leading to improper stowage
- Failure to declare dangerous goods
- Loading defective goods
- Providing incorrect handling instructions
- Failing to provide necessary documentation

This exception applies only where the shipper's act or omission caused the loss. If both the shipper's fault and the carrier's negligence contributed, the exception may not fully protect the carrier, or damages may be apportioned.

9.4.9 Other Exceptions

The remaining exceptions cover various specific perils:

War and enemies (rules 2(e) and (f)): Acts of war and public enemies cover damage from military operations, piracy, and similar hostile acts. Modern piracy raises questions about whether pirates are "public enemies" and courts have generally held that organised piracy qualifies.

Government action (rule 2(g)): Arrest, restraint, or seizure by government authorities excuses the carrier. This includes customs seizures, quarantine detention, and requisitioning of vessels or cargo.

Labour disturbances (rule 2(j)): Strikes, lockouts, and labour stoppages excuse delays and damage resulting from these events. However, the carrier must prove the loss was caused by the labour disturbance, not by the carrier's failure to take reasonable protective measures.

Lat***ent defects (rule 2(p)):*** Defects in the vessel not discoverable by due diligence excuse the carrier. This complements the seaworthiness obligation - if defects exist despite due diligence, the carrier is not liable for resulting damage.

General exception (rule 2(q)): "Any other cause arising without the actual fault or privity of the carrier" is a catch-all exception for causes not specifically listed. However, it requires proof that the carrier was not at fault. It is not a general escape clause.

9.5 Limitation of Liability

9.5.1 The Package and Kilo Limitations

Even where the carrier is liable (no exception applies), Article IV rule 5 of the *Hague-Visby Rules* limits the amount of liability. As implemented in Australia, the limitation is: "666.67 units of account per package or unit, or 2 units of account per kilogram of gross weight of the goods lost or damaged, whichever is the higher."

The "unit of account" is **the Special Drawing Right (SDR)** as defined by the International Monetary Fund. The SDR is a basket of currencies, and its value fluctuates against individual currencies. For Australian proceedings, SDRs must be converted to Australian dollars at the relevant exchange rate.

The carrier calculates limitation by:

1. Determining the number of packages/units or the weight in kilos
2. Calculating 666.67 SDRs x number of packages/units
3. Calculating 2 SDRs x number of kilos

4. Taking the higher amount
5. Converting to Australian dollars

For high-value cargo, these limitations are often far below actual value. For low-value bulk cargo, limitation may exceed value, making it irrelevant.

9.5.2 What Constitutes a "Package"

Determining what constitutes a "package" is critical for calculating limitation. Article IV rule 5(c) addresses containers: where goods are consolidated in containers, pallets, or similar articles, the packages or units enumerated in the bill of lading as packed in the article are deemed packages.

This prevents carriers from treating an entire container as one "package" with a single limitation amount. If a bill states, "container said to contain 100 cartons," the 100 cartons are the packages, and limitation is 100 x 666.67 SDRs, not 1 x 666.67 SDRs.

However, if the bill merely states "1 container" without enumerating contents, courts may treat the container as one package, drastically limiting the carrier's liability. This creates tension between the carrier's inability to verify container contents (requiring "shipper's load and count" qualifications) and the need to enumerate packages for limitation purposes.

Australian courts have examined this issue. In *El Greco (Australia) Pty Ltd v Mediterranean Shipping Co SA* [43], the Federal Court considered what constitutes adequate enumeration. The court emphasised that to obtain per-package limitation, the bill must clearly identify the number of packages within containers.

For non-containerised cargo, a "package" is generally what a reasonable person would consider a package - a shipping unit. Loose items may be individual packages, or groups of items might constitute packages depending on how they are packaged and shipped.

9.5.3 Weight Limitation

---

[43] [2004] FCA 202

The alternative limitation is 2 SDRs per kilogram of gross weight. Gross weight includes packaging. For heavy, low-value cargo, the per-kilo limitation may be lower than per-package limitation, and the carrier can limit to the lower amount (though the rule requires taking the higher, so effectively per-package applies).

For light, high-value cargo (electronics, jewellery, precision equipment), the per-package limitation will almost always exceed the per-kilo limitation. The 666.67 SDRs per package provides meaningful limitation for such cargo.

Weight-based limitation is primarily relevant for bulk cargo shipped without discrete packages, or for very heavy packages where the per-kilo calculation might somehow exceed per-package (which is rare given the 666.67 to 2 ratio).

9.5.4 Declaration of Higher Value

Article IV rule 5(a) allows shippers to declare higher value, in which case the carrier is liable up to the declared amount. The declaration must be "inserted in the bill of lading" and usually requires the shipper to pay higher freight based on the higher value.

In practice, declarations of higher value are relatively rare. Shippers often prefer to insure cargo rather than declare higher value, as insurance may be cheaper and more comprehensive than increased carrier liability. However, declaration of value can be useful for extremely valuable cargo or where insurance is difficult to obtain.

If value is declared, the carrier's limitation is the declared amount, not the package/kilo formula. However, the carrier can dispute whether the declared value is genuine or whether actual loss reaches the declared amount.

9.5.5 Loss of Right to Limit

Article IV rule 5(e) provides that the carrier loses the right to limit liability if damage resulted from "an act or omission of the carrier done with intent to cause damage, or recklessly and with knowledge that damage would probably result."

This high standard requires proof of deliberate or reckless misconduct. Ordinary negligence, even gross negligence, does not deprive the carrier of limitation. The cargo owner must prove:

- The carrier (or servants/agents) acted intentionally to cause damage,

OR

- The carrier acted recklessly AND knew damage would probably result

"Recklessly with knowledge" means more than should have known. It requires actual awareness of the likely consequences combined with deliberate disregard of that risk.

As discussed in Chapter 8, deliberate delivery without bills of lading may constitute conduct depriving carriers of limitation rights. Courts have held that fundamental breaches of the contract going to its root may fall outside limitation provisions.

In Australian law, the question is whether the conduct is so inconsistent with the contract that limitation clauses should not apply. This is a developing area, with courts carefully distinguishing between ordinary breaches (where limitation applies) and fundamental breaches (where it may not).

9.6 Time Bars and Notice Requirements

9.6.1 Notice of Loss or Damage

Article III rule 6 of the *Hague-Visby Rules* requires cargo owners to give notice of loss or damage to the carrier. Unless notice is given:

- Within three days of delivery (for damage not apparent at delivery), or
- At the time of delivery (for apparent damage)

The carrier is prima facie presumed to have delivered goods as described in the bill.

This notice requirement protects carriers by ensuring prompt notification of claims. It allows carriers to investigate while evidence is fresh and prevents stale claims where evidence has degraded.

"Apparent" damage means visible or detectable by reasonable examination at delivery. If damage is hidden within packaging or not discoverable without opening containers, it is not apparent, and the three-day rule applies.

Australian courts strictly enforce notice requirements. Failure to give timely notice does not bar claims entirely but shifts evidential burden. The carrier is presumed to have delivered goods in good condition unless the cargo owner proves otherwise.

9.6.2 The One-Year Time Bar

Article III rule 6 also provides an absolute time bar: "In any event the carrier and the ship shall be discharged from all liability whatsoever in respect of the goods, unless suit is brought within one year of their delivery or of the date when they should have been delivered."

This one-year period is absolute and cannot be extended by agreement (though it can be extended by mutual agreement after the claim arose). It runs from:

- The date of delivery, or
- The date when delivery should have occurred (for total loss or non-delivery)

The time bar applies to all claims arising from carriage under bills of lading - shortage, damage, delay, misdelivery, etc. It is jurisdictional, and courts cannot hear claims commenced after the period expires.

In *Akai Pty Ltd v People's Insurance Co* Ltd [44], the High Court of Australia examined time bar provisions in insurance contracts governed by the Marine Insurance Act 1909 (Cth). While this case concerned insurance rather than carriage, the principles regarding strict interpretation of time bars apply similarly to the Hague-Visby Rules.

"Suit" means formal legal proceedings. Pre-litigation correspondence, negotiations, or arbitration notices may not constitute "bringing suit" sufficient to comply with the time bar. Claimants must actually commence court or arbitration proceedings within one year.

---

[44] (1996) 188 CLR 418

Complications arise in multi-party disputes. If a cargo owner sues within one year but later seeks to add parties or amend claims, whether amendments relate back to the original filing depends on procedural rules. Prudent practice is to identify all potential defendants and causes of action within the one-year period.

9.6.3 Extensions and Tolling

The one-year time bar can be extended only by agreement of the parties after the cause of action has arisen. Article III rule 6 states:

"However, this period may be extended if the parties so agree after the cause of action has arisen."

Pre-claim agreements to extend time are void. Article III rule 8 prohibits any agreement relieving or lessening carrier liability otherwise than provided in the Rules. But once a claim has arisen, the parties can consensually extend time for bringing suit.

Extensions are common in practice. Parties often engage in negotiations and prefer to reach settlement without litigation.

If negotiations continue beyond one year, prudent practice is to:

- Commence protective proceedings before one year expires (which can be stayed pending negotiations), or
- Obtain written agreement from the carrier extending time.

Agreements to extend should be clear, in writing, and signed by authorised representatives. Informal or ambiguous discussions may not constitute valid extensions.

Australian civil procedure laws may provide some tolling of limitation periods in specific circumstances (such as minority or legal disability), but these generally do not override the contractual one-year time bar in bills of lading governed by the Hague-Visby Rules.

9.7 Himalaya Clauses and Extension of Protection

9.7.1 The Problem of Third-Party Claims

The *Hague-Visby Rules* protect carriers from liability, but what about independent contractors, stevedores, terminal operators, and other parties who handle cargo? At common law, cargo owners could sue these parties in tort, avoiding the carrier's contractual limitations.

This created an undesirable situation where carriers had limited liability, but their contractors faced unlimited exposure. It also created incentives for cargo owners to sue contractors rather than carriers, disrupting commercial relationships.

9.7.2 Himalaya Clauses

To address this problem, carriers include "Himalaya clauses" in bills of lading. These clauses extend the bill's protections (exceptions and limitations) to servants, agents, and independent contractors.

A typical Himalaya clause provides:

"Every servant, agent and independent contractor of the carrier (including every independent contractor from time to time employed by the carrier) shall have the benefit of all provisions herein benefiting the carrier as if such provisions were expressly for their benefit; and in entering into this contract, the carrier, to the extent of these provisions, does so not only on its own behalf but also as agent and trustee for such servants, agents and independent contractors."

The effectiveness of Himalaya clauses was established in *Scruttons Ltd v Midland Silicones Ltd* [45] and *New Sealand Shipping Co Ltd v A.M. Satterthwaite & Co Ltd (The Eurymedon)* [46], leading English cases followed in Australia.

These cases held that despite privity of contract doctrine, third parties can claim benefits under Himalaya clauses if:

- The bill clearly intends to benefit the third party

---

[45] [1962] AC 446

[46] [1975] AC 154

- The carrier contracted as agent for the third party
- The third party performed services in connection with the goods
- The third party's conduct constituted acceptance of the benefit

Australian law recognises Himalaya clauses. The *Civil Law (Wrongs) Act 2002 (ACT)* and similar legislation in other Australian jurisdictions also provide statutory frameworks allowing third parties to claim benefits under contracts in certain circumstances.

9.7.3 Scope of Protection

Himalaya clauses typically extend to the third party:

- All exceptions available to the carrier
- All limitations on liability
- All time bars and notice requirements
- Exclusive jurisdiction or arbitration clauses

However, protection is not unlimited. Third parties must act within the scope of their employment or engagement. If a stevedore deliberately damages cargo or acts outside authorised duties, Himalaya protection may not apply.

Australian courts examine whether the third party was acting in connection with the contract of carriage and whether their conduct fell within the scope of protection intended by the clause. In *Port Jackson Stevedoring Pty Ltd v Salmond & Spraggon (Australia) Pty Ltd (The New York Star)* [47], the High Court of Australia considered the scope of Himalaya protection for stevedores.

9.8 Both-to-Blame Collision Clause

9.8.1 The Collision Liability Problem

When two vessels collide, maritime law provides that if both are at fault, liability is apportioned between them. However, in some jurisdictions (particularly the United States), cargo owners on one vessel can sue the other vessel for the full amount of cargo damage, and that vessel then claims contribution from the first vessel.

---

[47] (1978) 139 CLR 231

This creates a situation where the carrier of the cargo may end up paying part of the cargo loss (through the contribution claim) even though it already faces liability to its own cargo under the bill of lading. The carrier effectively pays twice - once to its cargo, and again through contribution.

9.8.2 The Clause

To address this, bills of lading contain "both-to-blame collision clauses" providing that if collision occurs due to fault of both vessels, cargo owners must indemnify the carrier for any liability to the other vessel.

A typical both-to-blame clause provides:

"If the ship comes into collision with another ship as a result of the negligence of the other ship and any act, neglect or default of the master, mariner, pilot or the servants of the carrier in the navigation or in the management of the ship, the owners of the goods carried hereunder will indemnify the carrier against all loss or liability to the other or non-carrying ship..."

The clause effectively provides that cargo owners cannot benefit from recovering against one vessel while their carrier avoids liability under the navigation/management exception. If the cargo owner recovers from the other vessel, they must compensate their carrier for any contribution the carrier must pay.

9.8.3 Validity and Interpretation

The validity of both-to-blame collision clauses has been questioned. They appear to shift to cargo owners risks that the Hague-Visby Rules place on carriers. However, courts have generally upheld them as not directly contradicting the Rules; they operate after the fact to adjust recoveries, not to exempt carriers from initial liability.

Australian courts follow the approach in *The Fal Estuary*[48], recognising both-to-blame collision clauses as valid commercial devices to address the peculiarities of collision liability.

---

[48] [1990] 2 Lloyd's Rep 191

9.9 General Average

9.9.1 The Principle of General Average

General average is an ancient maritime principle: if cargo or ship is deliberately sacrificed to save the common adventure from peril, all parties (shipowner and cargo owners) contribute proportionally to the loss.

For example, if cargo is jettisoned to lighten a grounding vessel, or if the vessel incurs expense for repairs at a port of refuge after collision, these are general average losses. All cargo owners contribute proportionally based on the saved value.

9.9.2 General Average Clauses in Bills

Bills of lading contain clauses requiring cargo owners to contribute to general average. A typical clause provides: "General average shall be adjusted, stated and settled according to York-Antwerp Rules 2016 at such port or place as may be selected by the carrier and as to matters not provided for by those Rules, according to the laws and usages of the Port of [location]."

The York-Antwerp Rules are internationally recognised rules for calculating general average. They establish what constitutes general average, how losses are valued, and how contributions are calculated.

When general average occurs, the carrier typically requires cargo owners to provide security (cash deposit or guarantee) before releasing cargo. The carrier then appoints average adjusters who calculate each party's contribution. Settlement may take years.

9.9.3 Relationship to Carrier Liability

General average is distinct from carrier liability under the bill of lading. Even if the carrier was negligent (and thus liable for cargo damage under the bill), general average contributions may still be owed if circumstances justified general average actions.

However, if the general average situation arose due to the carrier's negligence or breach of duty, some jurisdictions hold that cargo need not contribute. This is a complex area where the interaction between general average principles and carrier liability creates difficult questions.

Australian courts recognise general average in accordance with international maritime practice, applying the York-Antwerp Rules as incorporated in bills of lading.

9.10 Interaction with Insurance

9.10.1 The Role of Marine Cargo Insurance

Given the extensive exceptions and limitations in carrier liability, cargo owners routinely purchase marine cargo insurance. Insurance covers:

- Losses exceeding carrier liability limits
- Losses falling within carrier exceptions
- Losses where carriers are insolvent or cannot be located
- Delays and other consequential losses not covered by carrier liability.

Marine cargo insurance operates on "all risks" or "named perils" bases.

Institute Cargo Clauses (published by the International Underwriting Association of London) provide standard terms. Clause A provides broad "all risks" coverage; Clauses B and C provide narrower "named perils" coverage.

9.10.2 Subrogation Claims

When insurers pay cargo claims, they are subrogated to the cargo owner's rights against the carrier. The insurer can sue the carrier in the cargo owner's name to recover amounts paid.

Subrogation claims must comply with all bill of lading requirements - time bars, notice provisions, and forum selection clauses. The insurer steps into the cargo owner's shoes and has no greater rights than the cargo owner had.

Australian law on subrogation follows general principles established in cases like *Castellain v Preston* [49]. The Marine Insurance Act 1909 (Cth) section 79 provides statutory recognition of subrogation rights in marine insurance.

---

[49] (1883) 11 QBD 380

9.10.3 Knock-for-Knock Agreements

Some trade sectors use "knock-for-knock" agreements where carriers and cargo insurers agree that each will bear their own losses without recourse to the other. This eliminates the cost and complexity of subrogation claims.

However, knock-for-knock arrangements require clear agreement and are not the default position. In the absence of such agreements, subrogation claims proceed normally.

9.11 Conclusion

The system of exceptions and limitations in bills of lading creates a complex but balanced risk allocation framework. Carriers must exercise due diligence and properly care for cargo but are not absolute insurers. Where losses occur despite proper care, or where excepted perils cause damage, carriers are protected. Even where carriers are liable, limitation provisions cap exposure.

This framework reflects centuries of maritime practice balancing the interests of carriers and cargo owners. The *Hague-Visby Rules*, as implemented in Australian law through the *Carriage of Goods by Sea Act 1991 (Cth)*, provide mandatory minimum standards while allowing some contractual variation.

Understanding exceptions and limitations is essential for all participants in maritime commerce:

Carriers must know their obligations, document their performance, and understand when exceptions apply. Proper record-keeping regarding seaworthiness, cargo operations, and casualty events is essential to defending claims.

Cargo owners must understand the limits of carrier liability and the importance of insurance. Notice requirements and time bars must be strictly observed or claims are lost.

Insurers must assess whether carriers have valid defences and whether subrogation claims are worthwhile. The interplay between carrier exceptions and insurance coverage determines ultimate loss allocation.

The next and final chapter examines contemporary issues and future developments affecting bills of lading, such as digitalisation, environmental concerns, and emerging challenges in modern shipping practice. The exceptions and limitations framework, as explored in this chapter, will continue to evolve but remains fundamental to maritime commerce.

Chapter 10: Contemporary Issues and Future Developments

10.1 Introduction

Bills of lading have demonstrated remarkable resilience over centuries of maritime commerce.

From medieval Mediterranean trade to modern container shipping, the basic functions - receipt, contract evidence, and document of title have remained constant. Yet the twenty-first century presents unprecedented challenges and opportunities.

To summarise:

- Digitalisation promises to revolutionise documentation.
- Environmental concerns are reshaping shipping practices.
- New technologies like blockchain, artificial intelligence, and autonomous vessels raise novel legal questions.
- Geopolitical shifts and changing trade patterns affect how bills operate.

This final chapter examines these contemporary issues and explores how bills of lading law and practice will likely develop in Australia and internationally.

Understanding these emerging challenges is essential because the bill of lading must adapt to remain relevant. If bills cannot accommodate technological change, alternative systems may replace them. If legal frameworks do not keep pace with commercial innovation, uncertainty and disputes will proliferate. Australian shipping law, like maritime law globally, must evolve while preserving the essential functions that make bills of lading work.

10.2 Digitalisation and Electronic Bills of Lading

10.2.1 The Imperative for Digital Transformation

The COVID-19 pandemic accelerated an already-growing push toward digitalisation in shipping. With offices closed and courier services disrupted, the inadequacy of paper-based documentation became glaringly apparent.

Industry estimates suggest that paper documentation costs billions annually in delays, courier fees, and inefficiencies.

Digital bills of lading promise substantial benefits:

- Instant transmission eliminating the late arrival problem
- Reduced costs from printing, courier, and document handling
- Enhanced security through encryption and authentication
- Better traceability and fraud prevention
- Integration with customs, port, and logistics systems
- Environmental benefits from eliminating paper.

The imperative is clear: digital transformation is not optional but essential for modern shipping.

The question is not whether bills will become electronic, but when and how.

10.2.2 Current State of Electronic Bill Adoption in Australia

Australia has participated in various electronic bill initiatives. Major carriers operating in Australian trades offer electronic bill options through platforms like Bolero, essDOCS, WAVE, and CargoX.

The Australian maritime industry has engaged with the Digital Container Shipping Association (DCSA) initiatives to standardise electronic bills.

However, adoption remains limited. Most Australian trades still use paper bills. Barriers include:

- Legal uncertainty about enforceability
- Limited participation across the shipping chain
- Banking sector conservatism
- Lack of interoperability between competing platforms
- Cost and complexity of implementation
- Resistance to change from established practices.

The Australian Government has expressed support for trade digitalisation.

The Simplified Trade System implementation plan recognises paperless documentation as a priority. However, specific legislation enabling electronic bills of lading has not been enacted.

10.2.3 Legal Reforms Needed in Australia

For electronic bills to achieve widespread adoption in Australia, legal reform is desirable though not absolutely necessary. The *Electronic Transactions Act 1999 (Cth)* provides general recognition of electronic documents but does not specifically address bills of lading as documents of title.

Recommended reforms include:

1. ***Explicit recognition in the Carriage of Goods by Sea Act 1991 (Cth):*** Amending section 11 to explicitly include electronic bills of lading, defining "possession" and "transfer" for electronic documents, and establishing functional equivalence between electronic and paper bills.

2. ***Adoption of UNCITRAL Model Law principles:*** The United Nations Commission on International Trade Law (UNCITRAL) has developed model laws on electronic commerce and electronic transferable records. Australia could implement these principles specifically for bills of lading.

3. ***Learning from other jurisdictions:*** The UK Electronic Trade Documents Act 2023 provides a statutory framework recognising electronic trade documents including bills of lading. Australia could adopt similar legislation, adapted to Australian circumstances and existing legislation.

4. ***Coordination with personal property securities law:*** Ensuring the Personal Property Securities Act 2009 (Cth) appropriately addresses electronic bills used as security interests.

Even without legislative reform, industry adoption through contractual frameworks may achieve practical electronic bill usage. However, legislation would provide certainty and facilitate universal adoption.

10.2.4 Blockchain and Distributed Ledger Technology

Blockchain technology offers particular promise for bills of lading because it provides:

- Unique digital tokens representing bills (solving the uniqueness problem)

- Immutable records of issuance and transfer
- Decentralisation eliminating single points of failure
- Transparency and traceability
- Smart contract capabilities for automated processes

Several blockchain-based platforms now operate:

- TradeLens (Maersk/IBM): Comprehensive platform including electronic bills
- CargoX: Blockchain bill of lading focused on neutral, interoperable system
- WAVE: Blockchain-based electronic bills with bank participation
- EdoxOnline: Platform for various trade documents including bills.

These platforms use different blockchain architectures (some permissioned, some public) and different technical approaches. The proliferation of platforms creates interoperability challenges – eg; a bill on one blockchain may not be recognised by parties using another.

Industry initiatives like the DCSA work toward standards enabling interoperability. However, universal standards remain elusive. The question is whether the market will consolidate around one or two dominant platforms, or whether interoperability protocols will emerge allowing multiple platforms to coexist.

10.2.5 Smart Contracts and Automated Processes

Blockchain enables "smart contracts", self-executing code that automatically performs actions when conditions are met. For bills of lading, smart contracts could:

- Automatically transfer bills upon payment confirmation
- Release delivery authorisation when bills are presented electronically
- Calculate and collect demurrage or detention charges
- Trigger insurance claims when loss conditions are detected
- Manage documentary credit transactions with automatic payment

Smart contracts promise efficiency but raise legal questions. If automated code executes a transaction based on incorrect data or programming errors, who is liable? Can smart contracts create binding legal obligations, or are they merely technical protocols? How do courts resolve disputes involving smart contract execution?

Australian law must grapple with these questions. The common law principle that contracts require intention to create legal relations suggests smart contracts can create binding obligations if parties intend them to. However, specific issues like error handling, dispute resolution, and regulatory compliance require development through case law or legislation.

10.2.6 Artificial Intelligence and Bills of Lading

Artificial intelligence (AI) is beginning to impact bills of lading in several ways:

1. ***Document processing:*** AI can extract data from bills, verify compliance with documentary credit requirements, identify discrepancies, and route documents through approval processes. This accelerates processing and reduces errors.

2. ***Fraud detection:*** Machine learning algorithms can detect patterns indicating fraudulent bills, unusual issuer behaviours, inconsistent data, or suspicious transaction patterns.

3. ***Predictive analytics:*** AI can predict delivery times, identify high-risk shipments, and optimise logistics based on bill of lading data.

4. ***Automated drafting:*** AI systems can generate bill of lading terms, select appropriate clauses, and customise terms based on cargo type and trade route.

These applications raise questions about liability when AI makes errors.

If an AI system approves a discrepant bill in a documentary credit, or fails to detect fraud, who bears responsibility? ..the bank using the system, the AI provider, or the human supervisor? Australian law will need to develop principles for AI liability in commercial contexts.

10.3 Environmental and Sustainability Concerns

10.3.1 Green Bills of Lading

Environmental consciousness is reshaping shipping. The International Maritime Organisation (IMO) has set targets for reducing greenhouse gas emissions from shipping by at least 50% by 2050 compared to 2008 levels. This drives demand for "green" or "sustainable" shipping options.

"Green bills of lading" are emerging, reflecting:

- Carriage on vessels using cleaner fuels (LNG, biofuels, hydrogen)
- Carbon-neutral or carbon-offset shipping
- Slower steaming to reduce emissions
- Optimised routing reducing fuel consumption
- Use of shore power in ports

Shippers increasingly demand carbon footprint information for their supply chains. Bills of lading may need to state:

- Vessel emissions profile
- Carbon footprint of the voyage
- Compliance with environmental standards
- Sustainability certifications

This raises questions about accuracy and verification. If a bill states cargo was carried on a "low-emission vessel" but this proves false, could cargo owners claim misrepresentation? Should carriers be liable for environmental statements in bills the way they are liable for statements about quantity and condition?

Australian environmental law may intersect with shipping documentation.

The *Australian Consumer Law* prohibitions on false or misleading conduct could potentially apply to environmental claims in bills of lading. As environmental, social, and governance (ESG) considerations become more prominent, legal frameworks will need to address green shipping claims.

10.3.2 Circular Economy and Bills of Lading

The circular economy concept of "minimising waste by reusing, refurbishing, and recycling materials" is gaining traction. This affects bills of lading for:

- Waste shipments for recycling
- Reusable packaging and containers
- Return logistics and reverse supply chains
- Extended producer responsibility schemes

Bills covering waste or recycling shipments may need special terms addressing:

- Classification and handling of waste materials
- Compliance with Basel Convention on transboundary waste movements
- Environmental liability if materials prove more hazardous than declared
- Tracking and chain-of-custody requirements

Australian participation in international waste trade regulation requires compliance with the Hazardous Waste (Regulation of Exports and Imports) Act 1989* (Cth) and related legislation. Bills of lading for waste shipments must reflect these regulatory requirements.

10.3.3 Climate Change Impact on Shipping Routes

Climate change is physically altering shipping. Arctic routes are becoming navigable for longer periods. Sea level rise affects ports. Extreme weather increases risks. These changes impact bills of lading:

1. ***Route flexibility clauses:*** Bills may include broader liberty clauses permitting alternative routes as traditional routes become impractical or new routes emerge.

2. ***Weather-related delays and exceptions:*** More frequent extreme weather may lead to more invocations of "perils of the sea" and similar exceptions.

3. ***Port substitution:*** Bills may need terms addressing delivery at alternative ports if climate change renders specified ports unusable (through sea level rise, storms, or ice).

4. ***Insurance and risk allocation:*** Climate change may affect how risks are allocated between carriers and cargo interests, potentially requiring evolution of exception and limitation provisions.

Australian courts may face cases involving climate-related shipping disruptions. The interpretation of force majeure, exceptions for acts of God, and reasonableness of route deviations may evolve to reflect new climatic realities.

10.4 Autonomous Vessels and Crewless Ships

10.4.1 The Coming Era of Autonomous Shipping

Autonomous vessel technology is advancing rapidly. Several jurisdictions are testing remotely controlled or fully autonomous vessels. While fully crewless ocean-going ships remain years away, the trajectory is clear.

Autonomous vessels raise fundamental questions about bills of lading:

1. ***The navigation/management exception:*** Article IV rule 2(a) of the *Hague-Visby Rules* excepts carrier liability for crew negligence in navigation or management. If there is no crew, how does this exception apply? Is algorithmic error equivalent to crew negligence? Who is the "master, mariner, pilot, or servant" when the vessel is controlled by AI?

2. ***Seaworthiness obligations:*** Article III rule 1 requires due diligence to properly man the vessel. For autonomous vessels, what does "manning" mean? Does it refer to the shore-based controllers or the algorithms and sensors?

3. ***Limitation of liability***: International conventions like the *Limitation of Liability for Maritime Claims Convention 1976* (as implemented in Australia) base limitation amounts partly on vessel tonnage and partly on assumptions about crewed operations. Will these frameworks apply to autonomous vessels?

4. ***Contracts and agency:*** Traditional maritime law treats the master as the carrier's agent with authority to make certain decisions and contracts. If there is no master on board, how are such matters handled?

10.4.2 Australian Regulatory Approach

Australia is actively exploring autonomous vessel regulation. The Australian Maritime Safety Authority (AMSA) has published guidelines for autonomous vessel trials. The *Navigation Act 2012* (Cth) and *Marine Safety (Domestic Commercial Vessel) National Law* provide regulatory frameworks but were drafted assuming crewed vessels.

Legislative reform will be needed to fully accommodate autonomous shipping. This includes:

- Safety standards for autonomous systems
- Liability frameworks for algorithmic errors
- Qualification and certification for remote operators
- Incident investigation protocols
- Cybersecurity requirements

Bills of lading law must adapt alongside these regulatory developments.

The Carriage of Goods by Sea Act 1991 (Cth) and the *Hague-Visby Rules* were drafted assuming traditional crewed vessels. While much of the framework remains applicable (cargo care obligations, exceptions for certain perils, limitation provisions), some provisions require reinterpretation or amendment.

10.4.3 Reinterpreting Traditional Provisions

Courts will likely apply purposive interpretation to adapt existing law to autonomous vessels:

1. ***Navigation exception:*** The purpose is to protect carriers from operational errors despite proper system design and maintenance. Algorithmic navigation errors might fall within this exception if the carrier exercised due diligence in developing and maintaining the autonomous system.

2. ***Seaworthiness:*** The obligation is to ensure the vessel is fit for its intended voyage. For autonomous vessels, this means ensuring autonomous systems are properly designed, tested, and maintained.

3. ***Fire exception:*** The Article IV rule 2(b) exception for fire not caused by "actual fault or privity of the carrier" should apply similarly for autonomous vessels. Fires from electrical faults or other causes remain excepted unless the carrier company was itself at fault.

However, some reinterpretation may stretch statutory language too far. Legislative amendment may be necessary to ensure clear legal frameworks for autonomous shipping.

10.5 Cybersecurity and Digital Risks

10.5.1 Cyber Threats to Shipping Documentation

As shipping digitalises, cyber threats increase. Potential attacks include:

- Fraudulent electronic bills of lading
- Hacking of shipping platforms to alter bills
- Ransomware attacks on carriers or digital platforms
- Man-in-the-middle attacks intercepting bill transfers
- Data breaches exposing commercial information

A successful cyberattack on a bill of lading platform could:

- Allow unauthorised parties to claim delivery of cargo
- Enable goods to be diverted to wrong destinations
- Compromise bank security in documentary credits
- Create chaos in global supply chains

10.5.2 Legal Frameworks for Cyber Risk

Australian law addresses cybersecurity through several frameworks:

1. ***Security of Critical Infrastructure Act 2018 (Cth):*** Designates certain assets (including some ports and shipping facilities) as critical infrastructure with enhanced security obligations.

2. ***Privacy Act 1988 (Cth):*** Requires notification of data breaches compromising personal information (though most bill of lading data is commercial, not personal).

3. ***Cybercrime legislation:*** The *Criminal Code Act 1995* (Cth) criminalises various cyber offenses including unauthorised access, data interference, and fraud.

However, specific liability frameworks for cyber incidents affecting bills of lading are underdeveloped. Questions include:

- If a platform is hacked and fraudulent bills issued, is the platform operator liable?
- If a carrier's system is breached and cargo misdirected, can the carrier invoke force majeure?
- If encrypted bills are decrypted through cyberattack, who bears the loss?
- What cybersecurity standards must parties meet to avoid negligence liability?

10.5.3 Cyber Clauses in Bills of Lading

Carriers are beginning to include cyber risk clauses in bills of lading:

- Excluding liability for losses due to cyberattacks
- Requiring cargo owners to maintain cybersecurity
- Allocating risk of electronic system failures
- Specifying notification procedures for cyber incidents

The validity of such clauses under the *Hague-Visby Rules* is uncertain. Article III rule 8 prohibits clauses lessening carrier liability below the Rules' standards. Can carriers exclude liability for losses caused by cyber incidents, or would this violate Article III rule 8?

The answer likely depends on whether cyber losses result from carrier breach of duty.

If a carrier fails to implement reasonable cybersecurity and cargo is lost due to hacking, the carrier may be liable despite exclusion clauses. If a sophisticated attack succeeds despite reasonable security, exclusion clauses may be effective as the loss arose "without actual fault or privity of the carrier" under Article IV rule 2(q).

10.6 Geopolitical Shifts and Trade Disruptions

10.6.1 Trade Wars and Sanctions

Geopolitical tensions create challenges for bills of lading. Sanctions regimes prohibit trade with certain countries, entities, or individuals. Carriers must ensure they do not carry sanctioned cargo or deliver to sanctioned parties.

Bills of lading increasingly include compliance clauses:

- Warranties that goods are not subject to sanctions
- Rights to refuse carriage if sanctions issues arise
- Requirements for cargo owners to indemnify carriers for sanctions violations

Australian sanctions law, primarily in the *Autonomous Sanctions Act 2011 (Cth)* and the *Charter of the United Nations Act 1945* (Cth)* implements UN and Australian autonomous sanctions. Carriers face criminal and civil penalties for sanctions violations.

If cargo is seized by authorities due to sanctions issues, questions arise about liability. Is this an excepted peril under Article IV rule 2(g) (arrest or restraint of princes)? Does the carrier have liability to cargo owners, or is the loss entirely the shipper's responsibility?

10.6.2 Brexit, Regional Trade Agreements, and Documentation

The UK's exit from the EU, new regional trade agreements like the Regional Comprehensive Economic Partnership (RCEP), and bilateral trade agreements create complexity. Different rules of origin, customs procedures, and documentation requirements apply depending on trade routes.

Bills of lading must accommodate:

- Multiple regulatory regimes
- Varying documentation requirements
- Origin declarations and certificates
- Customs documentation integration

Australia's trade agreements with various partners create different requirements for Australian exports and imports. Bills must be flexible enough to satisfy diverse regulatory requirements while maintaining core functions.

10.6.3 Supply Chain Resilience and Regionalisation

The COVID-19 pandemic and subsequent supply chain disruptions have prompted reassessment of globalised supply chains. Some predict "regionalisation, and shorter supply chains with more regional production.

If global supply chains shorten and regionalise, this might:

- Reduce the importance of long-term documents-in-transit situations
- Increase use of shorter-distance carriage where document arrival is less problematic
- Shift some trade from sea to air or land, affecting the dominance of ocean bills

However, predictions of deglobalisation may prove exaggerated.

International trade continues to grow, and maritime shipping remains the most cost-effective mode for many goods. Bills of lading will likely remain central regardless of supply chain configurations.

10.7 The Continuing Relevance of Bills of Lading

10.7.1 Alternative Documentation

Various alternatives to traditional bills of lading exist:

- Sea waybills: Non-negotiable documents avoiding some bill of lading complexities
- Delivery orders: For split shipments or when bills unavailable
- Cargo receipts: For simple acknowledgments without negotiability
- Electronic shipping records: Digital equivalents without full document of title character

Some predicted bills of lading would become obsolete as alternatives proliferated. This has not occurred. Bills remain dominant in international trade because:

- Document of title function essential for sales in transit and trade finance
- Established legal frameworks and market understanding
- Integration with documentary credits and banking systems
- Security for financing and insurance

10.7.2 Evolution Rather Than Obsolescence

Rather than becoming obsolete, bills of lading are evolving:

- Electronic bills replicating functions in digital form
- Smart bills with embedded digital capabilities
- Green bills incorporating environmental information
- Flexible bills accommodating multimodal transport

The essential functions - receipt, contract evidence, document of title remain necessary. The form and medium may change, but the functions persist because they serve fundamental commercial needs.

10.7.3 The Centrality of Legal Certainty

Bills of lading's continued relevance depends on legal certainty. Parties must be confident that:

- Bills will be enforced according to their terms
- Transfer of bills effectively transfers rights
- Courts will resolve disputes predictably
- International recognition ensures bills work across jurisdictions

Australian law, through the *Carriage of Goods by Sea Act 1991 (Cth)* and extensive case law, provides this certainty. Maintaining and enhancing legal certainty as bills evolve is essential to their continued centrality.

10.8 Reform Proposals and Future Directions

10.8.1 The Rotterdam Rules Revisited

The Rotterdam Rules, adopted in 2009 but not yet in force, represent the most comprehensive attempt to modernise maritime carriage law. They address:

- Door-to-door multimodal carriage
- Electronic transport records with detailed frameworks
- Updated carrier liability balancing interests
- Maritime performing parties and their liabilities
- Volume contracts for large shippers

Australia has not ratified the Rotterdam Rules and shows no immediate intention to do so. Concerns include:

- Increased carrier liability compared to Hague-Visby Rules
- Complexity potentially creating litigation
- Limited international adoption reducing benefits of uniformity
- Uncertainty about interaction with existing law

However, some Rotterdam Rules provisions, particularly those on electronic documents, could inform Australian domestic reform even without ratification. Selective adoption of beneficial provisions while maintaining the Hague-Visby framework might be possible.

10.8.2 UNCITRAL Initiatives

The United Nations Commission on International Trade Law (UNCITRAL) continues work on electronic commerce and trade facilitation. The Model Law on Electronic Transferable Records provides principles for electronic equivalents of bills of lading.

Australia could implement UNCITRAL principles specifically for maritime transport documents. This would provide legal certainty for electronic bills without requiring comprehensive reform of the substantive liability regime.

10.8.3 Industry Self-Regulation and Standards

Much innovation occurs through industry self-regulation. The Digital Container Shipping Association (DCSA) has published standards for electronic bills of lading. The International Chamber of Commerce develops rules for documentary credits and trade practices.

Australian participation in these industry initiatives helps shape global standards while ensuring they work for Australian trades. Public-private partnerships between government, industry, and legal professionals can drive effective reform.

10.8.4 Australian-Specific Reforms

Specific reforms that could benefit Australian shipping law include:

Explicit recognition of electronic bills: Amending the Carriage of Goods by Sea Act 1991 (Cth) to define electronic bills and establish functional equivalence with paper bills.

Clarification of multimodal carriage: Addressing the legal uncertainty around combined transport documents and clarifying the application of the Hague-Visby Rules to different segments.

Updating limitation amounts: The SDR amounts in the Hague-Visby Rules date from 1979. Consideration could be given to whether they remain appropriate.

Harmonisation with state laws: Ensuring consistency between Commonwealth maritime law and state-based commercial law on matters like sale of goods and security interests.

Environmental integration: Developing frameworks for environmental statements in bills and related liability.

Cybersecurity standards: Establishing minimum cybersecurity requirements for digital bill platforms and allocating cyber risk.

10.9 The Role of Education and Capacity Building

10.9.1 Legal Education

As bills of lading evolve, legal education must keep pace. Australian law schools should ensure maritime law curricula address:

- Electronic bills and digital transformation
- Emerging technologies (blockchain, AI, autonomous vessels)

- Environmental and sustainability issues
- International frameworks and comparative approaches
- Practical skills in drafting and dispute resolution

Continuing legal education for practicing lawyers, judges, and arbitrators should cover developments in shipping law, ensuring expertise remains current.

10.9.2 Industry Training

Shipping industry participants - carriers, forwarders, port operators, customs officials need training on:

- Legal principles governing bills of lading
- Electronic bill platforms and procedures
- Regulatory compliance including sanctions and environmental law
- Risk management and claim handling
- New technologies and their implications

Australian maritime organisations, industry associations, and educational institutions can collaborate to provide training programs ensuring industry competence.

10.9.3 International Cooperation

Bills of lading operate in an international context. Australian reforms and practices should consider:

- International standards and best practices
- Compatibility with major trading partners' systems
- Participation in international organisations (IMO, UNCITRAL, ICC)
- Learning from other jurisdictions' experiences
- Contributing to global development of maritime law

Australia's position as a significant maritime nation with sophisticated legal infrastructure allows it to contribute to international maritime law development while ensuring Australian interests are protected.

10.10 Conclusion: The Enduring Importance of Bills of Lading

Bills of lading have served maritime commerce for centuries, adapting continuously to changing technologies, trade patterns, and commercial needs. The fundamental functions - providing receipts for goods shipped, evidencing contracts of carriage, and operating as documents of title remain as essential today as in medieval times.

The twenty-first century presents unprecedented challenges:

- digitalisation demanding new legal frameworks,
- environmental concerns reshaping shipping practices,
- technological innovations from blockchain to autonomous vessels, and
- geopolitical shifts affecting trade.

Yet these challenges also present opportunities. Electronic bills can solve long-standing problems like late document arrival. Smart contracts can automate complex processes. Green shipping can address climate imperatives while creating new markets.

Australian shipping law has demonstrated adaptability, from implementing the *Hague-Visby Rules* to accommodating containerisation and modern commercial practices. The legal framework established by the *Carriage of Goods by Sea Act 1991 (Cth)* and developed through judicial decisions provides a solid foundation. This foundation must evolve to address contemporary challenges while preserving the legal certainty that makes bills of lading work.

The key challenges for Australia include:

- Providing clear legal recognition for electronic bills of lading
- Ensuring frameworks accommodate new technologies while managing risks
- Balancing carrier liability with legitimate commercial needs
- Addressing environmental and sustainability concerns
- Maintaining international competitiveness and alignment with global practices

The key opportunities include:

- Leading regional adoption of digital bills and related technologies

- Developing sophisticated legal frameworks that other jurisdictions may emulate
- Strengthening Australia's position as a maritime nation and trading economy
- Creating efficiencies that benefit all participants in maritime commerce
- Contributing to global maritime law development

Bills of lading will remain central to international trade because the functions they serve - documenting shipments, establishing contractual relationships, enabling goods to be traded in transit, and providing security for financing are fundamental to commerce.

The medium may shift from paper to digital, the technology may incorporate blockchain and AI, the specific terms may evolve to address new risks, but the essential character persists.

For students, practitioners, and policymakers, understanding bills of lading means appreciating both the historical foundations and the contemporary developments. The principles established over centuries, obligations regarding seaworthiness and cargo care, exceptions for perils beyond carrier control, limitations balancing liability with economic viability remain sound. Yet these principles must be applied and adapted to new contexts.

As we conclude this examination of bills of lading in shipping law, several themes emerge:

- ***Continuity and change:*** Core functions persist while forms and technologies evolve.

- ***Balance of interests:*** Effective law balances carrier, cargo owner, financier, and public interests.

- ***International character:*** Bills operate globally, requiring harmonisation while accommodating local variations.

- ***Commercial pragmatism:*** Law must serve commercial needs while maintaining principle.

- ***Adaptability:*** The system must evolve with shipping practice, technology, and societal values.

The bills of lading of 2050 may be entirely digital, embedded with smart contracts, tracked on blockchains, and carried on autonomous vessels.

Yet they will still serve the same essential purposes:

- documenting what was shipped,
- establishing the terms of carriage, and
- enabling commerce through negotiable documents representing goods in transit.

The legal principles examined in these chapters - issue and transfer, receipt statements and evidential effect, contract formation and incorporation of terms, document of title character, delivery obligations, exceptions and limitations will remain relevant, though perhaps applied in new contexts.

Australian shipping law, grounded in statute, elaborated through case law, and informed by international practice, provides the framework for bills of lading to continue serving maritime commerce well into the future. The challenge and opportunity for Australia is to ensure this framework evolves appropriately, maintaining the security, certainty, and efficiency that make bills of lading indispensable to international trade.

For all who study, practice, or engage with bills of lading, from shipping law students to seasoned maritime practitioners, from cargo insurers to trade finance bankers, from shipping company executives to Australian policy makers, the message is clear: bills of lading are not relics of the past but living instruments at the heart of global commerce, continuously adapting to serve the timeless need to move goods across oceans while managing the commercial, legal, and documentary relationships that carriage creates.

The journey through these ten chapters from introduction through functions, types, issue and transfer, receipt and contract evidence, document of title character, delivery obligations, exceptions and limitations, to contemporary challenges has traced both the established principles and the emerging developments.

This knowledge equips readers to navigate the complex world of bills of lading in Australian and international shipping, to understand disputes and transactions, to draft effective terms and manage risks, and to contribute to the continued evolution of this essential instrument of maritime commerce.

LIST OF ABBREVIATIONS

ACL	Australian Consumer Law
AGLC	Australian Guide to Legal Citation
AMSA	Australian Maritime Safety Authority
ANU	Australian National University
CIF	Cost, Insurance and Freight
CIP	Carriage and Insurance Paid To
CMR	Convention on the Contract for the International Carriage of Goods by Road
COGSA	Carriage of Goods by Sea Act
CPT	Carriage Paid To
Cth	Commonwealth (of Australia)
DCSA	Digital Container Shipping Association
EDI	Electronic Data Interchange
ESG	Environmental, Social, and Governance
FCA	Free Carrier
FCR	Federal Court Reports
FOB	Free On Board
IMDG Code	International Maritime Dangerous Goods Code
IMO	International Maritime Organization
Incoterms	International Commercial Terms
LOI	Letter of Indemnity
MTO	Multimodal Transport Operator
NSWLR	New South Wales Law Reports
NVOCC	Non-Vessel Operating Common Carrier
PPSA	Personal Property Securities Act
QB	Queen's Bench
RCEP	Regional Comprehensive Economic Partnership

SDR	Special Drawing Right
SOLAS	International Convention for the Safety of Life at Sea
UNCITRAL	United Nations Commission on International Trade Law
UCP	Uniform Customs and Practice for Documentary Credits
UK	United Kingdom
UKHL	United Kingdom House of Lords
VGM	Verified Gross Mass
VR	Victorian Reports
WLR	Weekly Law Reports

ABOUT THE SERIES

INTERNATIONAL TRADE AND TRANSPORT LAW LIBRARY

The International Trade and Transport Law Library provides comprehensive analysis of the legal frameworks governing international commerce and maritime transport. Each volume combines authoritative Australian legal perspectives with international conventions, comparative approaches, and practical applications.

Written for legal practitioners, shipping professionals, trade finance specialists, and students of commercial law, this series bridges the gap between academic scholarship and professional practice.

Published by John Gates Books, each volume draws on the author's unique perspective as both a former Naval Officer and practicing International Trade and Transport Lawyer.

BOOKS IN THE SERIES:

Book 1: ***International Trade – the Ins and Outs of Import and Export,*** published 2014, rev 2026
Book 2: Bills of Lading in Shipping Law
Book 3: [Title - forthcoming]

Made in United States
Orlando, FL
04 November 2026

90200308R00128